Updraft/Downdraft

Secondary Schools in the Crosswinds of Reform

Marilyn Crawford
Eleanor Dougherty

A SCARECROWEDUCATION BOOK

The Scarecrow Press, Inc.
Lanham, Maryland, and Oxford
2003

A SCARECROWEDUCATION BOOK

Published in the United States of America
by Scarecrow Press, Inc.
A Member of the Rowman & Littlefield Publishing Group
4501 Forbes Boulevard, Suite 200, Lanham, Maryland 20706
www.scarecroweducation.com

P.O. Box 317
Oxford
OX2 9RU, UK

British Library Cataloguing in Publication Information Available

Library of Congress Cataloging-in-Publication Data
Crawford, Marilyn, 1947–
    Updraft/downdraft : secondary schools in the crosswinds of reform / Marilyn
Crawford, Eleanor Dougherty.
    p. cm.
    "A ScarecrowEducation book."
    Includes bibliographical references.
    ISBN 0-8108-4569-5 (alk. paper)—ISBN 0-8108-4570-9 (pbk. : alk. paper)
    1. Education, Secondary—United States. 2. School improvement programs—
United States. 3. High school teaching—United States. I. Title Updraft,
downdraft. II. Dougherty, Eleanor, 1947–III. Title.
LA222 .C73 2003
373.73—dc21
                                                                        2002011767

⊗™ The paper used in this publication meets the minimum requirements of
American National Standard for Information Sciences—Permanence of Paper
for Printed Library Materials, ANSI/NISO Z39.48-1992.
Manufactured in the United States of America.

The battle over standardized testing pits the good of the many against the good of the (powerful) few, challenging the very premises of our democratic thinking.

—James Traub 2002

Contents

Prologue: Why Not?   vii

1 "Hammering on Cold Iron"   1

2 Updraft/Downdraft   11

3 What Are Artifacts and Why Use Them?   29

4 A High School Case Study   39

5 Analyzing Calendars, Student Schedules,
and Master Schedules   61

6 How to Analyze Curriculum and Instruction   81

7 Creating Updraft for All—Bold, Bolder, Boldest!   97

Epilogue: Noah's Beauty   111

Bibliograpy   125

Appendix 1: Collecting Information   129

About the Authors   131

Prologue: Why Not?

Anne C. Lewis

American public high schools, especially those in urban areas, resemble a terminally ill patient on a regimen of experimental cures. For several years, the commentary, reports, studies, and calls for reform of high schools have used self-congratulatory terms such as "radical" or "revolutionary" to describe their ideas. Many share the same themes such as breaking up high schools into smaller units, focusing on applied learning, giving students options, and/or linking with community resources.

The proposals also share two characteristics: They are disconnected, and they are too timid.

The authors of this volume expertly document the failure of high schools to respond to the circumstances, needs, and futures of most of their current students.

Statisticians studying dropout rates come to different conclusions, but they all agree that the dropout rate from high schools is at least 15 percent, and in urban high schools it is triple that number or greater. Our secondary schools lose at least 800,000 young people every year, a number that has not changed very much in two decades of education reform.

Before the 2001–2002 recession, we already had more than five million youth, ages 16–24, who could not find a job, even with a high school diploma, because they lacked skills or those skills needed for employment in their area. Almost half were white youth.

We are fooled into thinking increased college enrollment is a barometer of better times in high schools. Only about half of the students who enter four-year college programs obtain a degree. Community colleges, which feel the brunt of underprepared students, lose half of enrollees before the sophomore year; only 6 percent go on to a baccalaureate degree. In fact, only seven states received a grade of A for their preparation of young people for college from the National Center for Public Policy and Higher Education in 2001. Twenty-seven received a grade of C or worse.

Meanwhile, the poor performance and leadership of urban districts has led to near-desperate attempts to make different governance arrangements. It's as if a sign were put up over urban districts like the discard bin at a garage sale—"take what you want, cheap."

In Baltimore, the mayor gave up direct control of the school board in favor of a state-mayor shared responsibility. The deal brought the city district more money; in three years, it has done little to improve student performance. In at least eight other urban districts, control of the schools reverted to mayors. In Philadelphia, a state takeover involves a controversial plan to turn over part of the district, and much of the central office, to a for-profit management company. Other state takeovers in the past decade may have improved fiscal operations and facilities; none produced significant improvement in student test scores. Researcher and policy consultant, Paul Hill, suggests a reconfiguration that would create charter school districts. Others believe vouchers to individual families would bring about urban district reform. None of these substitute arrangements have proof of success behind them.

The picture of mostly poor and/or minority students languishing in impersonal and irrelevant school settings, if the students are there at all, contrasts dramatically with examples of contexts in which students in difficult environments become engaged learners. These are places that listen to students. They vigorously link learning to relevant opportunities and to the students' communities. They use all resources possible to support the transition of young people to the adult world. Unlike many schools, these are places where youth want to be.

You can find engaged students in alternative out-of-school programs such as YouthBuild, inside small career academies within regular high schools, or participating in non-school activities provided by community-based organizations, for the most part. Some attend community-designed public schools such as El Puente in New York City.

What these small successes share are: supportive, small communities of learning that balance academics with youth development; ties to the community; and purpose in young people's lives. Most importantly, they involve more than one institution in students' lives. A city's full resources are considered potential partners, mined and integrated into a support system around young people.

Such examples exist right in the face of traditional educators and the policymakers who support them. Except for career academies, the places that have the most potential to help students learn are not part of the mainstream and are marginalized. Little in the way of a policy framework exists to connect them systemically. How many English teachers, for example, know that down the street their students are giving public drama performances that they have spent weeks preparing for, or are taking part in community poetry slams?

The Youth Advisory Councils under the Workforce Investment Boards in urban areas gave city leaders an opportunity to create comprehensive education and support systems around young people. They don't break with past perceptions of "training," however, and few of them have been able to overcome lack of funding and prestige.

After spending much of the past seven years documenting school reform in urban districts, primarily for foundations, I now believe that the only hope for urban high schools, and perhaps whole districts, is to start all over. The current system for educating urban youth cannot be healed without wasting another generation, spending a great deal of additional money, and relying on only limited improvements to keep the momentum going.

What cities and their youth need are a new vision, a new governance arrangement, and citywide responsibility for supporting youth into adulthood. If city leaders opted to start all over, one can envision a truly radical youth education system built on positive values, collaboration, and accountability for results.

After sufficient time for researching ideas, planning, and construction—based on considerable and widespread community involvement, especially by students and their families—the old district, on the stroke of a midnight bell, would cease to exist and in its place would be:

- A citywide policy board representing each educating institution in the community including the schools, cultural institutions, recreation organizations, community colleges and other higher education institutions, libraries, businesses, social service agencies, and

community-based organizations, as well as city government. It
would be supported by an advisory board representing educators,
parents, and students from each high school. They would jointly
develop a communitywide vision for the education of all youth that
integrates academic and youth development goals, and each partner would be evaluated regularly as to the quality and results of
their participation.

• Collaborative agreements that would arrange for sharing personnel,
  budgets, and facilities for functions that involve the education of
  youth. Corporate training centers, for example, would extend career training started in small learning communities in the high
  school building. Art, music, and drama instruction would involve
  large blocks of time for students at cultural facilities in the community. Library personnel would be linked to research/project tasks
  of students. Community college classes would be available in high
  school buildings. As in some European countries, exceptionally tal-
  ented athletes and performers would spend part of their learning
  time at recreational and cultural centers.

• An accountability system involving all of the partners. Businesses
  that provide internships, for instance, would agree to performance
  criteria for their participation/supervision. Higher education institutions would have a synergistic relationship with the schools in
  many ways—preparing and supporting teachers as coaches/brokers
  for a new system, opening up resources for advanced students, en-
  hancing community support systems—and be held accountable for
  results.

• A structure of options for students that encourages them to hold
  high expectations and standards for themselves. Upon certification
  that they have achieved adequate skill levels, they would opt for
  other small learning communities with career and academic orien-
  tations. They would continue their academic work in these settings,
  but also use the community as a learning place. Advanced students
  could choose early college entrance or independent study. All students would be expected to be involved in service and/or problem
  solving for their communities. Students needing extra time to complete basic work would have it—in the regular system and as a
  standard choice rather than a stigmatized one. Community-based

organizations would be part of the team, included in on policy-making as well as decisions involving supports for individual students.

Each urban jurisdiction would need to work out the details that suit it best. The important step is to free secondary education from its constrictions and think big; big enough to recognize the complexity of influences on young people and harness the rich resources that exist in every urban area. High school students are closer to adulthood than to childhood. They need lots of opportunities to work alongside adults in purposeful learning that allows them to know what it means to do quality work and to make a contribution.

The details, however, probably will stump most readers—until they start thinking out of the box. Why have a superintendent? Wouldn't an instructional CEO and a management CEO be able to work together? Why should teachers be afraid of such a change? They would not lose collective bargaining, though current contracts might be abrogated to allow the re-employment of teachers, provided they agreed to participate in high-quality professional development and be accountable for results with students. Think of the possibility of saving in areas where high schools and communities duplicate services (e.g., libraries, vocational shops, some specialty teachers). Think of the larger pool of creativity and leadership available when people across services and communities are allowed to break out of their boxes and collaborate at all levels.

In many ways, these ideas are not radical. All of them exist in some way or place. There are full-service schools that bring community resources to students, certificate of mastery initiatives, career academies linked to local businesses, service learning and independent study initiatives, arts in the schools, and higher education options for advanced students. The ideas and efforts percolate in lots of places. An education system that works for the twenty-first century would bring all of them together into an overall vision and a policy/governance framework that supports the full development of our young people. Moreover, it would place communities of families, students, and local leaders at the center of designing and monitoring the transition of youth.

When I first began thinking of this new system several years ago, I discussed it briefly with John Gardner. I was concerned that if the planning were not done smartly, the result could be an even greater behemoth of bureaucracy around kids than now exists. "Don't worry," he said. "Even if problems develop 20 years down the road, this transformation will have shook up the establishment to a point where it could never go back to old ways."

So, why not?

1

"Hammering on Cold Iron"

We want to learn about where we came from, places like China and Russia and Africa, not just European countries.

—Sacramento high school student

The great American educator of the nineteenth century, Horace Mann, said that the teacher who attempts to teach without inspiring students to learn is "hammering on cold iron." His comment recognizes that the partnership between teaching and learning is unassailable. Most people who spend their days inside schools know instinctively what research confirms, that the correlation between effective teaching and student achievement gains is a fact, as well as the correlation between weak teaching and student failure. Students who experience high demand and support as well as challenging curriculum and instruction build toward success in school and opportunity in life after school. In contrast, those who experience ineffective teaching lose not only content and skills but time and opportunity.

Current school reform has tried to change the predictable outcomes of the past by shifting the blame away from poverty or students and parents to what is or isn't happening inside schools. According to the National Commission on the High School Senior Year (2001), the "primary goal of high schools should be graduating students who are ready and eager to learn more, capable of thinking critically, and comfortable with the ambiguities of the problem-solving process." Yet, secondary schools face the job of accomplishing the Commission's goal inside a larger social system where students do not share the same high support and quality educational experiences. Historically, students achieve within the secondary system along socio-economic and racial lines.

1

The path of differentiating students' academic experiences around more challenging and meaningful work in the K–12 years starts with expectations about learning and about who can learn to high standards. Differences in expectations can be stark, as this woman reveals after visiting her neighborhood public school to decide whether to send her daughter there or to a private school.

> "They discussed reading by age nine," Ms. Clements, a Princeton-educated marketing consultant, said later. "I thought, really? We're trying to get them to read by the time they're four." (Bannon 2001)

Secondary schools get pressure to differentiate expectations for students not only from inside the school but also from outside as the social and economic stakes loom larger near the end of the K–12 continuum. Parent groups, business, and social institutions have played their part in cementing the belief that some students "want" to learn and others don't, and indeed there are differences in pressure:

> Parents, teachers, and administrators in Scarsdale, New York, made a collective decision over the last few years that they would pay as little attention to the tests as possible. Scarsdale could afford to do this because the culture of the schools is the exact opposite of the culture that has brought standards-based reform into being: the internal pressure to succeed according to the highest standards is so intense that external motivations are superfluous. And so in the eighth-grade English class I sat in on at the Scarsdale Middle School in the weeks leading up to the E.L.A. test, the kids were wearing masks and cloaks and performing a scene from "Romeo and Juliet," which they planned on studying for a good eight weeks. (Traub, p. 60)

Vocal groups of parents, such as those in Scarsdale, have proven how powerful they can be when they pressure the district to shape opportunities to learn in their students' favor (Powell 2001; Hartcollins 2001). Likewise, a group of Maryland parents decried the district's attempts to extend the language arts period in middle schools because they felt that their students didn't need more reading despite low reading test scores on the state assessment (Johnson 2001). A series in *The Washington Post* found that Montgomery County, Maryland, a suburban district with a wide range of economically and racially diverse populations, housed schools with widely different educational experiences determined largely by the class of the population, according to the authors. Some descriptions underscore how affluent and poor schools differ in the daily routines of schooling. One example is an economically advantaged school where elementary students are greeted with classical music each morning. These third graders study algebra and parents raise money to upgrade computers. In Montgomery County, as in other districts, real estate prices ride on the performances of schools and set sale prices accordingly. The series claims that houses in neighborhoods where students score high on the SAT sell for double the price of houses with the exact same plan in another school area where SAT scores are lower (Shulte and Keating 2001).

> **E-mail to Author**
>
> I have a marginal interest in other kids and only after I'm assured that mine have what they need. That is not perhaps the "right" attitude, but I think it is the one that prevails. Until you can convince me that this can be a win-win, nothing will change, and you won't get my vote.

Money alone does not seem to be the key to student achievement, however. Low performing schools often suffer from poor management of time and resources despite the influx of state and federal dollars. They tend to depend on substitutes and uncertified teachers. Faculty display defeatist attitudes, and classrooms are home to instructional chaos. Instead of focusing on quality of instruction, low performing schools tend to make order and discipline the priority at the expense of academic achievement, squelching attempts to improve instruction because such attempts are bound to call for change and some disruption. Low performing schools value harmony over disharmony because leadership does not know how to manage periods of flux on the way to flow. A veteran music teacher in a high poverty middle school with persistently low performance related to one author how he had a rule at home never to ask him how his day went. The lack of leadership at the school and district over the years had made teaching impossible. He said that he felt so unprofessional that the only way he had survived was not to have to admit to his family how poor his teaching had become inside such a culture of low expectations and accountability.

If different expectations for different students take root in elementary schools, middle and high schools seal the pact. Although the current reform is committed to transforming schools into places where all students have access to high quality curricula and instruction, secondary schools remain largely impervious to two decades of reform. (Elementary schools are beginning to show progress in larger numbers.) The reason why, we suggest, is that the secondary school is a complex place where dynamics designed to withstand pressures from inside the educational community and outside have evolved over time. Precisely because of its unique complexity, reform requires complex action—no single solution will work. To improve student achievement, we believe that secondary schools must understand the dynamics—historical, operational, and pedagogical—that cause effective and ineffective teaching.

In the high school years, achievement has traditionally been expressed in terms of credits and GPAs. In the current standards-based reform, students must meet standards and pass assessments. In either system, learning takes on an intensity and importance unlike other years in school. Because high school bridges childhood to adulthood, the outcomes of grades and credits matter and shape the future. Learning takes on an urgency as students speed through four years of courses toward graduation and into their young adult lives. For some, that next step is college or university, community college or technical school. For others, it is work or the military. And, for others, incarceration or joblessness.

> During 1999, only 54 of every 100 young adults lacking a high school diploma or a GED certificate were employed, versus 75 of every 100 high school graduates and nearly 89 of every 100 four-year college graduates. Among black high school dropouts, only 23% held full-time jobs. (Herbert 2001)

Pressures like these lead us to think that the two most pertinent questions in this book for leadership are (1) What is leadership doing to make teaching possible and the best it can be? and (2) What is leadership doing to make learning to high standards possible for all students? The methods described in *Updraft/Downdraft* provide leadership with tools for making the invisible forces that perpetuate the sorting and selecting of students clearer. Armed with these tools, then, leadership can better create the infra-structures involving the use of resources and time to achieve equity.

HIGH SCHOOL AS A CULTURAL MIRROR

If you hold up a mirror to the secondary school experience, especially high school, you will see corollary pressures operating inside the school reflective of those inside the larger society. The same sorting and selecting dynamics that exist in communities also exist in secondary schools. Perhaps because high school is the last common institutional experience offered in our society before we are let out to the more clearly competitive world of college and the workplace, we relate to high school with a certain intensity. Or perhaps because our economic, civic and intellectual well-being as a country depends in large part on the successful bridging of adolescence to adulthood that begins in secondary school, we—individually and institutionally—are all bound to the secondary experience.

Hardly anyone reacts to the mention of high school neutrally. Memories of high school conjure up the good and the bad, a host of experiences during adolescence that have inspired a range of cultural venues. Song, literature, and film have explored the yin and yang of these critical years ever since the comprehensive public high school emerged on the American scene some hundred and fifty years ago. Something about high school penetrates the American cultural psyche with a sharpness that makes many squirm.

Popular literature and movies have captured our feelings about the high school experience in tales of high school truants, overaggressive prom dates, revengeful geeks, and teachers pushed to their limits. Undoubtedly, the experiences that people have during high school have fed the American psyche to such an extent that it has taken a prominent place in popular culture. One theme contrasts how the generations remember or experience high school differently, for better or worse, as does Sinclair Lewis's character, Babbitt, in the novel of the same name. Babbitt remembers his pre-war years in high school through rose-colored glasses. "From the memory of high-school pleasures back in Catawba, he suggested the nicest games: Going to Boston, and charades with stew-pansfor helmets, and word games in which you were an Adjective or a Quality." In contrast, Babbitt's son struggles with high school, a dilemma that Babbitt finds perplexing.

The high school pressures its own culture with social and political forces that affect the educational experience. Inside this culture, these forces conspire to determine who has access to the experiences and contexts that support the level of learning that is needed to gain access to the next step, postsecondary education. Historical data shows us that, indeed, secondary education has prepared the middle and professional classes of students, largely consisting of white students, for this next step. For this group, secondary experiences support a positive and confident view of life and its possibilities. Such students "get the message" that college or some postsecondary institution is a given, and the curriculum, teaching and homework demands underscore that message alongside family or community supports.

For others, high school falls into two general experiences: painful or irrelevant. "It was a struggle"; "High school wasn't for me"; "Just didn't like it"; "No one knew I existed"; "Can't remember a single teacher's name"; and "Worst years of my life" are just some of the descriptors collected in a casual survey. For those who struggle with the academic, social and political forces inside high schools, the mere mention of "high school" connotes frustration and alienation. In the book *Geeks* Jonathan Katz captures such experiences in his chronicle of two students whose educational and social isolation is palpable. Rejected by their peers and teachers, these boys turn to the Internet for conversation, knowledge, and connections to other worlds. Through the Internet, not human contact, they find their way to a future in Chicago. Likewise, in *Hope in the Unseen,* Ron Suskind follows a black Washington, D.C. inner-city

Letter from College, 1945

Hi, folks! My grades this time aren't going to be as good as usual, I'm afraid. My hygiene teacher gives whatever grade happens to pop in his head, and the last time he popped me a B+ and that was one of the highest but he didn't like my last paper and the old goon gave me a D. Imagine that, me! And I knew just as much about the stuff as lots of people that got B's and C's. Now that's just preparing you gently and it's not going to be my fault altogether 'cause everybody says he doesn't grade fair and now I believe it. Love and kisses, Bettye (Author's mother's letter to parents from college, 1945) high school student whose attempts to negotiate the system are often curtailed by unresponsive adults.

Movies are particularly good at capturing the attitudes many have about high school, mostly irreverent and satirical. *Ferris Bueller's Day Off*, a near cult classic with teens, satirizes just about everything high school has to offer and portrays high school as a waste of time for anyone who can think. In *Clueless* the heroine, Cher, approaches her teachers to get her C raised to an A in the same way one might negotiate a sales deal since she views actually doing her assignments as generally unnecessary.

One image resonates in particular. In the 1984 dark comedy about high school, *Teachers,* students drudge dutifully into history class every day, pick up the daily ditto sheet on their way to their desks, spend the class period completing the sheet, and then drop it off into a box on their way out. The teacher, a quintessential burned-out type, sits at his desk reading the newspaper. One day a student notices that the teacher hasn't moved in days and discovers he has died. This scene rings true with anyone who has had burned-out teachers, and everyone can relate to the boredom of classroom instruction that is unimaginative and routine.

Inside the media culture, the "failing school" story appears frequently in the news, in documentaries and feature articles, putting images of serious problems in front of the education community and the general public alike. Some examples include "Bush's Teacher Plan Falls Short" and "Go to the Back of the Class Grade Inflation Conceals that Schools Are Failing Our Kids." In concurrence, national data confirm problems of dropouts, grade inflation, unqualified teachers, and many other long-rooted problems. "Part of the reason for the poor performance of American students is structural." In a critical editorial (3/26/2000), Jack Kelly of *The Pittsburgh Post-Gazette* goes after schedules, school calendars and poor teaching. "The 3 Rs largely have been supplanted by psychobabble. But the major problem is the greed and incompetence of teachers and school administrators." Why our schools struggle to educate all students has become news worthy, if not sometimes strident and accusatory.

In the last decade, public policy has moved toward establishing a framework for creating schools that delivers what successful students have always had: a quality education buttressed by high supports and expectations, interesting lessons and resources. Such students are primed to learn and bring with them intellectual energy. They accept the challenge of an essay on "scholarship" or a geometry proof. They are fairly confident that they can get what they want from high school, and that the adults inside and outside the school are supporting them in their efforts to succeed. Successful students have benefited from a strong high school curriculum and accountability. We know that a rigorous math curriculum, for example, improves achievement, and that a college preparatory curriculum benefits low performers. Yet, national research tells us that though 72 percent of high school students graduate with a diploma, only a third of those graduate from a four-year college. Like Babbitt, parents who worry when students show signs of struggle in their coursework know what's at stake.

It was Ted who most worried Babbitt . . . . With conditions in Latin and English but with a triumphant record in manual training, basket-ball, and the organization of dances, Ted was struggling through his Senior year in the East Side High School. (Sinclair Lewis, *Babbitt,* 1922)

That high school experiences differ is a persistent theme in popular culture and in the research about secondary education:

High school consists of essentially two different worlds, one preparing students for college, the other preparing adolescents for the workplace at best, and for nothing in particular at worst. (Sedlack, Wheeler, Pullin, and Cusick 1986)

The academic implications of a strong or weak high school education often do not impose themselves in students' lives until after graduation, a day when the vast majority of students receive a diploma as indication of their persistence in high school. However, students may well find out that their diplomas do not represent adequate skills, knowledge and practices when put to the test in college or in the workplace. Only 26% graduate in five years with a BA. Ethnically, African American, Latino and Native American persistence in college is substantially lower than Asian or Anglo. (Education Trust 2000)

High school, then, mirrors society-at-large which pressures the high school to serve its economic, political and social masters. Like other cultures, the secondary culture is difficult to change. Our aim, though, is not so much to know the culture as to work our way through aspects of the culture in an effort to discern if our schools are providing excellence, equity and access to all students. If not, to provide the data high school and central staff need to make critical choices and decisions.

In this book, we offer a variety of ways to look more closely at the challenging context in which secondary teaching occurs, making visible the unseen forces that either support secondary teachers in holding high expectations for all, or constrain them and inadvertently create "updraft/ downdraft" dynamics in their classrooms:

In chapter 2, we review the research on holding high expectations in secondary schools that gives insight into how updraft/downdraft dynamics operate in the classroom, and how they impact teachers and learners. The research synthesis helps us better understand the conflicting pressures that are ever present as a function of the two distinct and conflicting roles that high schools are expected to perform. Much of this information in the form of research and analysis has been in the education journals since the '80s and is not new. This information is, however, vastly underutilized in the world of practice. By examining the evidence from research, we can follow a trail that leads to clarification of the context in which teaching and learning are nested in practice.

In chapter 3, we move from the world of external research to discuss tools schools can use to conduct their own inquiries, moving directly into the world of practice. We introduce the concept of "artifacts" as sources of data that help schools and districts make visible their own updraft/downdraft pressures. Artifacts such as school master schedules, student schedules, course selection documents, and other items can be used to monitor expectations pushed by the system—are all students expected to learn at high levels, or are some expected to succeed while others fail?

In chapter 4, we show how an urban high school used artifact analyses to learn more about the context that impacted teacher ability to teach with greatest effectiveness. Through this case study, we show how a secondary school used the analyses of artifacts to show the strength of updraft/downdraft forces versus high expectations for all, with a brief discussion of the action the school took to offset those negative dynamics.

Chapters 5 and 6 offer schools and districts a series of strategies for conducting self-analyses using a variety of types of artifacts. In chapter 5, we look at artifact analysis related to use of time, talent, and energy for learning and teaching. And in chapter 6 we look at artifact analysis related to curriculum and instruction. In both, we include guiding questions as well as practical tools for creating data that give insight into the dynamics of holding high or low expectations in your own setting.

In chapter 7, we share "bold, bolder, and boldest" responses to updraft/downdraft dynamics, pushing schools to think both of what is, and what might be as we work together to create schools that work for all. And, finally, in an Epilogue by Terry Roberts and Laura Billings, we visit a Paideia classroom to see what hearty secondary classrooms might look like if, and only if, we decide as a nation to make "updraft" for all.

2

Updraft/Downdraft

To an important extent, people tend to live up (or down) to what is expected of them.

—Rutter, Maughan, Mortimore, Ouston, and Smith 1979

The lesson of the Power of Context is that we are more than just sensitive to changes in context. We're exquisitely sensitive to them.

—Malcolm Gladwell 2000

Every day high schools engage in a process of selecting and sorting students that results in some students receiving the education and supports that will lead them into the college path while others receive a very different education, one that trades off behaviors for a diploma. The latter students experience, on a daily basis, low-level expectations accompanied by low-level courses and assignments. They learn that if they show up to school and do the minimal work, they will receive a diploma. At this point, unlike their counterparts who are looking ahead to a rigorous postsecondary education, their vision of an education ends.

We describe these two contrasting and conflicting experiences as a system caught in an "updraft" and a "downdraft." The updraft/downdraft description of secondary education takes its cue from a broader societal experience about social class. It describes how we shape the very lives of children and adolescents through a process called "social reproduction," a term used to describe the re-creation of the existing class strata from one generation to the next. Additionally, our history of differentiating school-

Seat Time and Order

"The little Asian boy was restless, getting up from his seat nine times. I counted. Every time he did, the teacher would say, 'Stanley, sit down. Go back to your seat.' After he got up the ninth time, a little black kid got up from his seat. The teacher turned to him and said, 'You're out of here!' "

When this was pointed out to the teacher, Ladson-Billings said, "She was shocked that she had been so inequitable. Part of it is this subconscious thing that you've got to control these black children. That's the biggest fear teachers exhibit in regard to black children."

To Ladson-Billings, a professor of education at the University of Wisconsin at Madison who also taught at Santa Clara University, the incident was neither surprising nor unusual.

It has led her and other educators to consider the profound impact of race in U.S. classrooms, how children respond to it, and how that response effects achievement.

"What (such treatment) says to them is that you're not here to be educated—you're here to put in seat time," said Ladson-Billings. (Nakao 1998)

ing experiences for African American, Latino, Native American, and ethnic groups further complicates this dynamic of sorting and selecting students into opposing educational pathways. National trend data track a persistent pattern of differentiating schooling experiences, so named the "achievement gap" between white and Asian students and their African American, Native American, and Latino peers. (Education Trust 2000).

Under the norms of social reproduction, students who enter kindergarten with social privilege tend to leave high school poised for privilege in the future, while those who enter school underprivileged tend to leave underprivileged. Thus, students of privilege are more likely to operate in an updraft that nurtures and supports high achievement, while underprivileged students more typically operate in a downdraft that presses them firmly toward low achievement.

Now schools, under new norms, are pressured to teach all students of all social class strata to achieve high standards. Under this system, all students are expected to exit high school armed with the necessary skills to succeed in postsecondary education and in a demanding workplace. Globalization and our new world economy presses hard on the need for an educated workforce, thus driving schools to provide a high quality education for all students. Unless we find ways to improve academic performance for all students, we will be unable to sustain strength as a nation. Because of this national need, strong public forces are pushing hard on social reproduction, and we have supports in place through policy and practice for taking on history.

At the same time, the institutionalized processes grounded in competition continue to have powerful support, particularly from those advantaged under that system. Why does this struggle impact our high schools in particular with such strength? High schools are the place where the rubber meets the road, as students move from the K–12 nest ready to fly— or crash—into the "real world." The high school journey is fundamentally competitive, as students jostle one another for excellence as measured by class rank, GPA, and SAT scores—the weaponry that lets top ranking students gain entrance into coveted postsecondary slots and access to a brighter future. As part of the path leading to scholarships and entrance into highly respected universities, grades and class rank can be converted to cash equivalent as students who excel in school advance to high-paying professional careers. This economy is strongly supported by many privileged citizens who are advantaged under the old system.

Under pressure to meet societal expectations, high schools catch the brunt of the disconnect in the two systems: strong forces support the "old" system as students compete for grades, the system that sorts, while at the same time other strong societal forces support the "new" system, designed to support high achievement for all. As you can well imagine, the clash between the old and the new is of titanic proportions, and secondary school reform reverberates from battle. The standards and accountability movement works in opposition to the updraft/downdraft pressure of social reproduction, and the old updraft/downdraft system and the new standards-based system are in fundamental conflict: (1) the old system tells teachers to sort students into categories of success and failure, and (2) the new system of standards and accountability tells teachers to demand that all students succeed.

A place where this conflict plays out in practical terms is around report cards. One Pennsylvania district has met for two years trying to come up with a standards-based secondary school report card. On the one hand, the report card has to communicate student progress within a system calling for traditional measures that are based on credits and A–F grades, usually spread along a bell-curve, and the other on meeting the standards. College admissions drive the need to maintain the old system. Meanwhile, high schools operate within a district standards-based system and are committed to "meeting the standards" language and policy. Report cards have yet to capture the two reporting demands at the high school level although elementary schools have generally managed to switch to standards-based reporting.

These two powerful, conflicting systems—the updraft/downdraft system of social reproduction and the high expectations-for-all system of standards and accountability—both find their way into classrooms and are ever present in impacting teacher ability to hold high expectations for student achievement. These strong yet opposing forces create conflicting backdrop for teaching that presses high school staff both to continue to sort and, at the same time, to educate all students to a high level of achievement. Both conflicting demands impact teaching and learning on a daily basis. Obviously, teachers are torn in attempting to meet the demands of both systems, regardless of the strength of pressure supporting each.

Secondary teaching is situated in this dual context, and, according to Joe Murphy (2000), "teachers cannot out-teach their context." Too often administrators, school boards, researchers, the public and even teachers, themselves, overlook this reality. Teaching is very much a factor of the conditions that enable or disable effective teaching. That is to say, teaching a heterogeneously grouped English class can benefit students if the class size is manageable, and the range of skills isn't too extreme. With appropriate resources, time, and support from other staff, teachers can take on the many challenges that secondary schooling demands of them. But without basic tools, for example appropriate professional development, collaborative planning periods, a wide range of reading materials, and support for special needs students, effective teaching becomes less and less possible. Even for the best skilled, most experienced teachers, there are those obstacles that can't be overridden. If all students are to receive the benefits of good teaching, then, the possibility for effective teaching must be true for all staff, not just for those teaching in the updraft. Context has the greatest power in inhibiting good teaching, or in freeing good teaching. No, context alone does not make a poor teacher better, but context can stop good teachers from doing their best to educate all students.

In this book, we offer a variety of ways to look more closely at the challenging context in which secondary teaching occurs, making visible the unseen forces that either support secondary teachers in holding high expectations for all or constraining them and inadvertently creating updraft/downdraft dynamics in their classrooms.

THE WORLD OF SECONDARY RESEARCH

The overarching intimate tie between schooling and the recreation of an occupational and economic hierarchy in each new generation has an overwhelming impact on daily school experiences, for teachers and students together. (Metz 1990)

The Honing Process

The process is well known. It starts on a child's first day of school and continues subtly throughout his or her academic career. Schoolchildren are tracked, sorted, labeled, and pigeonholed. Some are chronically detained, expelled, suspended, or removed. Either they are "pushed out" or they are graduated knowing little. Either way, they have failed and been failed.

The honing process creates public schools that look very much like demographic prisons, with the least preferred children holding the short straw—and with the career path between schools and prisons becoming all too direct. The process is grounded in our often subliminal perceptions of children according to race, class, religion, sex, disability, and demeanor, and is acted out by teachers, administrators, and others. Then, it is legitimized with arguments for greater discipline and instructional serenity. (Casserly 1996)

Since the early 1990s, standards and assessments brought on by Goals 2000 have set the stage for the decade and beyond. Yet, while assessments and state accountability systems tell high school teachers to hold all students to high standards, grades and class rank continue to tell teachers to sort students into categories of success and failure. We can use the research to look inside this fundamental split and to analyze how this split happens and becomes entrenched.

Research on high schools is synthesized in the book *The Productive High School* (Murphy, Beck, et al. 2001), a qualitative analysis of the research on U.S. high schools. Much of the research summarized in this chapter is taken from the portion of that work which helps us understand the high school's role in social reproduction, and why societal forces so strongly impact high expectations for student achievement. By following the literature's story, we can begin to better understand why high schools are so resistant to changing the updraft/downdraft system. And, on the more positive side, we can begin to gain information that helps us unlock new sources of power and wisdom for improving high schools so they work for all.

Dual Paths, Differentiated Expectations

The updraft/downdraft phenomenon creates two separate tracks—dual paths to students' differentiated futures. As we discussed in the introduction, teachers and students operate in context of a wind shear—one force a clear updraft that drives high achievement, the other a strong downdraft that actually drives low achievement. This wind shear flows through every crack and crevice of secondary schools and classrooms. Some students ride the updraft to success, while others plummet predictably into an undertow of low achievement.

How do the dual paths to differentiated futures begin? Starting in the middle school years, placement differences seem to be mediated through systemic differences in the overall speed and direction of achievement that (1) increasingly limit program options, and (2) influence student choice. These differences are linked to students' ultimate purpose in obtaining a high school education:

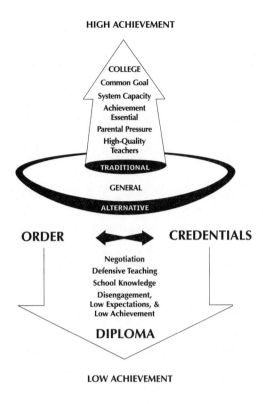

HIGH ACHIEVEMENT

COLLEGE
Common Goal
System Capacity
Achievement
Essential
Parental Pressure
High-Quality
Teachers

TRADITIONAL

GENERAL

ALTERNATIVE

ORDER ◄──► CREDENTIALS

Negotiation
Defensive Teaching
School Knowledge
Disengagement,
Low Expectations, &
Low Achievement

DIPLOMA

LOW ACHIEVEMENT

Figure 2.1
Updraft/Downdraft

Rather than being propelled through the same curriculum at different speeds . . . students are pulled intentionally through different curricula toward different "end points": different high schools, different post-high school expectations . . . . The differentiated curriculum conforms to larger social purpose—preparing students for different futures—and creates even greater curricular differences than would be expected from differences in pace and consequent losses in coverage. (Oakes and Lipton 1996)

Thus one compelling message in the research tells us that differentiated expectations pull the system, and students along with it, deliberately and forcefully into separate tracks.

Life in the Updraft

Those of us reading this book probably have participated in some up-draft scenarios. Perhaps it was a time when our parents helped us polish off an essay or design a science fair exhibit. Updraft students know very well how to establish good relations with teachers and by high school use it to their advantage. One adult related how, as a senior, she experimented with an English teacher. She didn't turn in an assignment but saw in his grade book that she had received an A. She had bet on her reputation as an A student to get an A even when she didn't do her work, knowing that the teacher probably didn't even read the papers and assigned grades based on his impressions of students. (Crawford and Dougherty)

While a clear understanding of how students are assigned to separate tracks at the high school level is ever-emerging, once students are either assigned to or elect to participate in different tracks, the evidence of track differences in the quality of instruction, curriculum, and learning environment is very strong. For the most part, students in different tracks have widely varying access to educational resources:

> The available evidence indicates that curriculum assignment, in addition to its sorting function, is an institutional mechanism for the systematic and selective allocation of important learning resources, systematic in that the allocation occurs in regular patterns and selective in that the resources are distributed in a different manner to various curricular groups. (Murphy and Hallinger 1985)

Thus lower-track high school students "with records of lower achievement are more likely to find themselves in classrooms that emphasize lower-order skills, repetitive drill techniques, and basic knowledge" (Lee et al. 1995, p. 5). High school students in higher-track classes—disproportionately white and Asian, disproportionately wealthy—access higher quality schooling.

As a result, in high track courses it is relatively easy for teachers to hold high expectations for student achievement, while in low tracks teachers assume that they don't have to expect the vast majority of students to meet rigorous standards. These radically different sets of expectations split high schools quite cleanly into distinctly different groups:

> Children of workers attend schools and are placed into educational tracks, both of which emphasize conformity and docility and prepare them for low-status jobs. By contrast, the sons and daughters of the elite are invited to study at their own pace under loose supervision, to make independent decisions and to internalize social norms—all of which prepare them to boss rather than to be bossed. (MacLeod 1995)

While the research gives us detailed information on how tracking occurs and provides research-based support for the vast differences in quality of the educational experience that exists in different tracks, the overall knowledge base on tracking is not news. We've known about this difference in student and teacher life in separate tracks for a long time, both through research as well as through our own personal jaunts through high school.

So what can we learn from the research that's new? Let's take a step closer, looking with more detail into the research to move beyond simplistic awareness of this dynamic. We need to go inside the evidence, to risk taking a closer

Grades as Cash Economy

Grouping and its consequences have meaning and exchange value beyond school. After all, homogeneous grouping, accompanied by public labels and status differences, signals which students should gain access to the university and the status and life chances that higher education can bring. Thus, tracking became part and parcel of the struggle among individuals and groups for comparative advantage in distributing school resources, opportunities, and credentials that have exchange value in the larger society. Therefore, it is not surprising that there were those with a clear personal stake in maintaining homogeneous grouping. (Oakes, Quartz, Ryan, and Lipton 2000)

look at this experience in search of greater understanding to better enable us to reconfigure and reform the high school. The first view, the updraft, is easy and familiar. The second, the downdraft, is more disconcerting and may well make us all feel distinctly uncomfortable. Let's start with the easier one—easier because it is probably most familiar to us all.

Some Students Experience Academic Updraft

The winds of high achievement are familiar and strong. When students, parents, and teachers—together—take serious action to prepare adolescents for college, a powerful updraft drives high achievement. All share a common goal. The adults in the system have the capacity to help students achieve that goal, and achievement is firmly nested in context of that goal. Achievement is essential to successfully reaching and completing the goal of postsecondary success—parents pressure the system for the best teachers and for access to high level courses; the best teachers gravitate toward the most ambitious students and the college-preparatory tracks; schoolwork has meaning for students because it is in context of their motivation systems; everyone engages in the effort and school basically works for these students in their ambition to gain access to college.

When updraft occurs, students are operating in school in context of powerful personal motivation systems that actually pull them toward high achievement. When students are clearly focused on college entrance and success, they are more likely to be motivated to engage in the hard work of learning and to achieve because much of high school is contextual. High school students are motivated when they believe school assignments are important and when they decide that achieving in school will move them ahead in the future. For students focused actively on college entrance and future success, high school coursework does both. When school is important and moves students toward a brighter future, achievement is nested in context of their motivation systems, and students are more likely to engage in the hard work of learning. In short, while we tend to think of high expectations as a system of "push," the research tells us it is also a very forceful system of "pull"—a system that pulls students to achieve through motivation, as well as the more traditional forces that push student achievement.

Other Students Experience Academic Downdraft

> Students have the opportunity to select courses comparable to individual abilities, talents, and career goals. The guidance department and the administration reserve the right to change a student's schedule based on past academic performance and standardized testing results and to accommodate the needs of the student body. (from a high school planning guide, 2000–2001)

For students focused solely on earning a diploma, however, the story research tells is quite a different matter. The dynamics are a little trickier to follow, but a large body of research strongly and clearly outlines the story. Let's take a look at the downdraft so we can better understand students and schools who fail to achieve in our secondary schools.

When high school students focus on earning a diploma as the ultimate goal of high school, strong forces actually drive low achievement—strong negative pressures that operate with forces equal and opposite to those in the updraft of the wind sheer. This downdraft is a function primarily of a high school diploma that has little societal value as a terminal credential, a fact that students recognize:

> Besides, I didn't really care to try in school . . . . You ain't got a chance of getting a good job, even with a high school diploma. You gotta go on to college, get your Masters and [expletive] like that to get a good paying job that you can live comfortably on. So if you're not planning on going to college, I think it's a waste of time. (A student, MacLeod 1995)

This downdraft is a condition rarely talked about or recognized in faculty meetings or school councils—even if students name it on their own terms everyday, often using pejorative words. Even though this dynamic is well documented in the research world, it has not become a mainstream part of the wisdom of practice.

We follow the path from the external world into the school, ending our journey inside the classroom. As you read, think about these questions— Why does this negative dynamic occur? How does it occur? What does it look like in the classroom? Where are the opportunities for improvement?

Three Forces Interact

This fundamental dynamic that drives low achievement, the downdraft, is a function o f three forces whirling in combination: (1) a diploma with little value as a final credential, (2) pressure to maintain order separated from focus on achievement, and (3) pressure to award credits for graduation separated from achievement. Under this system, powerful forces are in play, but achievement is not one of them.

Three forces interact to create this pressure for low achievement, beginning with the context set by a diploma of little value to society and moving on to the negotiation that occurs within that context—a trade-off driven by the need to maintain order and the need to earn credits for graduation:

1. Weak Diploma

The high school diploma as a terminal credential offers little reason for students and teachers to engage in the hard work of learning. When students are aggressively focused on postsecondary success, achievement in school is in context of their motivation systems, as we discussed earlier. When students are focused solely on earning a diploma, however, school—and achievement—is out of context, and students have little reason to see achievement in school as important to their lives now, nor do they have reason to believe high school alone offers them possibilities for a brighter future. When students' eyes are on the diploma alone, they have little reason to engage in the hard work of learning because the diploma has little societal value. In short, pressure to earn a diploma is dissociated from pressure to achieve.

2. Pressure to Earn Course Credit

In order to earn a diploma, students must collect an Easter basket full of course credits—with particular number of eggs of appropriate colors. By doing what teachers ask—an eclectic mixture of doing homework, taking tests, turning in daily assignments, participating in class, doing extra credit assignment, attending—students are able to earn course credit.

When pressure for earning grades and graduating is the core focus, students often find that they can do well in school even if they give minimal effort:

Within a belief system in which all that counts is graduation—in which earning good grades is seen as equivalent to earning mediocre ones, or worse yet, in which learning something from school is seen as unimportant—students choose the path of least resistance. (Steinberg 1996)

Thus, requirements for earning course credit have always been, and in many instances continue to be, separate from more pure measures of achievement. This separation is particularly strong in courses that are not aligned with demanding postsecondary context, where achievement is naturally embedded in the course itself. When courses are out of context of demand for high achievement, students can earn credit that allows them to pass without demonstrating high levels of achievement by meeting minimum requirements.

Uphill Teaching

As high school teachers, we have experienced what it is like to have the system come down hard. Both of us in separate states and in very different high schools felt the pressure to conform to a code of order when we tried, to name a few incidences, to take students into the community, teach topics that students argued about, or group students across tracks for a Socratic seminar. In both our cases, we had to "deal" to get our way. That meant in one case passing on the credit for achievement gains to the principal in exchange for being "left alone." In the other case, buying off the principal with expensive wine. (Crawford and Dougherty)

3. Pressure to Maintain Order

When teachers maintain relatively quiet classrooms and send few students to the office, they are given high degrees of autonomy by the system even though they may be maintaining order by demanding little of students academically.

What administrators wanted were teachers who liked and related to the students, who had few discipline problems, or who at least handled those they had themselves. Beyond that it seemed that they asked little of the teachers, leaving them alone as individuals to work out their own pattern of instruction, patterns that went unscrutinized as long as there was no trouble or rumor of trouble in their classes. (Cusick 1983)

When classrooms churn, however, the system comes down hard on the teacher to restore order, often with little regard to focus on achievement as a priority.

Under the old system, these three forces—pressure to maintain order and pressure to award course credit in context of a weak and relatively valueless credential—interact to create a powerful downdraft that drives low achievement through negotiation.

Negotiation

This downdraft is created through a classic and well-documented trade-off that occurs quietly and predictably in high school classrooms across the country when system pressure to maintain order and to award credit is separated from strong systemic demand for achievement. Through a process of negotiation, teachers and students actually trade credits for maintaining order and thus create a downdraft that drives low achievement:

- First, teachers lessen their demands for academic work, for time on task, or for conformity (Metz 1993).
- Second, students agree to play the game without making trouble for the teacher (Newmann 1985).

How can this happen? Again, the research tells a powerful story. Because teachers are the gatekeepers who control the awarding of credits, they control access to the diploma. As a function of sheer volume, students have a strong voice in maintaining an orderly classroom environment. When we look at these two pressures together, we see that teachers are pressed (1) to award credit and (2) to keep order, while students are pressed (1) to earn credits and (2) to maintain order. So, under the old system, students and teachers literally barter—order the students' bargaining chip, credentials the prerogative of the teacher—and a cycle that leads to low-level academic knowledge is firmly established.

While this dynamic may seem surprising in its starkness, the research goes on to tell us several interesting things:

- That bartering is "normal" for the old context in which it occurred, the context that promotes sorting. Each teacher and learner approaches the classroom on the basis of a personal assessment of costs and rewards. Bargaining, which lies at the core of the classroom (or any organizational or human relationship) is not an aberration from the norm and cannot be eliminated through more rational administrative processes. (Sedlack et al. 1986)
- That bartering is situational, rather than being an all-or-nothing phenomenon. Most of the teachers observed used a combination of teaching styles and strategies. Some taught defensively only when they felt threatened by a particular administrative policy (detracking), by a certain group of students, or by lack of confidence with the course material or more open instructional methods. (McNeil 1986)

When bartering is the basic classroom dynamic, the results are predictable—bartering leads to defensive teaching, defensive teaching leads to "school knowledge," school knowledge leads to disengagement, low expectations, and low achievement.

Defensive Teaching

When teachers use teaching strategies focused primarily on maintaining order and awarding credit, we can get a closer look inside this vortex of negative achievement and see how teaching takes on a defensive stance inside classrooms. Teaching strategies focused on order and credentialing are known as "defensive teaching." Examples of defensive teaching strategies include:

- Ignoring students who are disengaged as long as they are reasonably quiet and non-disruptive.
- Letting students work for long periods of time on individualized projects with low demand and little guidance.

- Focusing on building good relations with students as the center-piece of curriculum rather than on achievement of a high level body of knowledge.
- Adjusting the learning process so that students become passive consumers of information rather than active learners.
- Assigning easy lessons so that students do not have to ask too many questions or require interaction with the teacher around content.
- Avoiding "controversial" topics or literature.
- Limiting the scope of instruction out of fear that learning might be noisy or disruptive.
- Controlling knowledge as a way of managing student behavior by addressing complex topics in a superficial way, using fragmentation and omission to simplify complex knowledge with mystery in order to close off discussion.

When teachers teach defensively, they create a phenomenon known as school knowledge:

> Defensive, controlling teaching does more than make content boring: it transforms the subject content from "real world" knowledge into "school knowledge," an artificial set of facts and generalizations whose credibility lies no longer in its authenticity as a cultural selection but in its instrumental value in meeting the obligations teachers and students have within the institution of schooling. (McNeil 1986)

School knowledge is distinct from both teacher and student personal knowledge of the world and is fundamentally uninteresting. In the English movie *Educating Rita,* Rita's tutor tells her that he isn't sure he wants to teach her to pass the exams because he knows she will lose some of the honesty and freshness of her essays, written in her Eastside London vernacular. He can teach her to write in the essayist style, he says, yet regrets that that also involves her having to squelch much of her personal knowledge and expression.

When school knowledge takes over the classroom, teachers control how knowledge is managed. They are the arbitrators of what is acceptable and what is not. Students who go along with the teacher and dutifully learn school knowledge are described by students as being "school smart," which means they "buy" the teacher's view of knowledge. Students' clarity about this kind of student and teacher should cue adults into the level of understanding students have about how teaching and learning can play out. They are particularly savvy about identifying teachers who teach them and those that do not. School knowledge, "content that neither the teachers nor the students take very seriously," (McNeil, p. 98), is a product of defensive teaching. School knowledge and defensive teaching, though expressed in student terms, are nevertheless transparent to students. The problem with such teaching and content is that it leads to disengagement.

Defensive teaching and school knowledge is, in the words of students, "boring." Often, teachers' defensive stance causes them to "water down course content and reduce their own teaching efforts [while] the students cooperate patiently in class, while silently negotiating how much course content to believe and remember after they were tested" (McNeil 1986). The stage, then, is set for a time-tested game that occurs between teacher and students.

Disengagement, Low Expectations, and Low Achievement

The bottom line? The dominant response to teaching for order is to significantly lower expectations for effort and achievement with both teachers and students disengaging from the work of teaching and learning. When teachers use negotiated teaching strategies and create school knowledge, both teachers and students are more likely to disengage rather than to engage in the work of learning and teaching.

- Adults who visit high school classrooms are often struck by the dullness of the lessons. Those who visit systematically note the overwhelming prevalence of boring content, dull presentations and bored but patient students (Goodlad 1984).
- "Dull presentations . . . not caused by poor teacher preparation or teacher burnout, but by deliberate, often articulated, decisions teachers have made to control students by controlling the content" (McNeil 1986, p. 191).

When this occurs, "students have even less reason to be engaged" (Metz 1993, p. 113) and pressure to disengage increases (Murphy, Beck, et al. 2001).

MOVING FROM RESEARCH TO PRACTICE

It's one thing to learn about "updraft/downdraft" from the research, yet it's quite another thing to see it in practice. In the next section, we guide you through an analysis of the updraft/downdraft dynamics you may find in your own school. By looking with an analytical eye at your own high school's artifacts, you will find a vast source of data—data quietly awaiting analysis—right at your fingertips. School artifacts, analyzed with care, offer a gold mine of information about the forces of differentiated expectations that may exist in your schools and classrooms.

3

What Are Artifacts and Why Use Them?

ar-ti-fact (är′ tə fakt′) *n.* *something made or modified by humans usually for a purpose*

"The test scores are in!" Word springs from desktop to desktop, and the superintendent and her assessment experts gather to open the long-awaited boxes that house the future. One by one the answers emerge; one school improves while another plummets; some results expected and others greeted with disbelief. Papers sprawl across the floor as the team works late into the night, the story emerging one pile at a time. Once the overall news is in, the team steps in to take a closer look, to see "which" students are learning—all? Some? If not all, then who? In addition, they ask "what" standards students are learning, and what standards they are failing to learn. In the end, the team has good news and bad, and they celebrate where reform is working but move quickly back to the drawing board to erase the failures and chase the all-consuming goal of making school work for all.

This scene plays itself out in districts across the country, as looking at results becomes more and more a part of the everyday lives of educators, parents, students, communities, and policymakers. Effective school leaders spend hour upon hour pouring over data in order to measure the impact of their work, to know if they hit their target of success for all. They ask tough questions and look for honest answers—Are our students learning? Do students from all social groups learn equally? Are we improving as a school? Are students attending? Do they stay in school and graduate? Do they go on to postsecondary schools, and do they finish that level with success? These are all very critical questions that drive school improvement—analyzing test data, attendance data, dropout/retention data. Using data to analyze school performance has become normal fare for schools working to improve, as well as for those outside schools who press for public school progress.

As important as looking at results is, it is not enough to use data to look primarily at the product of the journey. Schools must look as well at the expectations and supports they are providing students and teachers as they move down the school pathway that leads to success or failure. If schools and districts are to learn to drive decisions with sound information, and if the public is to skillfully demand ongoing improvement, all must learn to think in much broader terms about what indeed constitutes "data."

WHAT ARE "ARTIFACTS"?

Secondary schools need to learn to analyze data to see if the updraft/downdraft dynamics are present in their own classrooms. In addition to the more familiar data sources such as test scores and dropout rates, strewn casually about schools are other important sources of data that we call artifacts. Readily available yet often unrecognized as data sources, these artifacts and other less tangible items can be used to monitor whether secondary schools are creating the updraft/downdraft phenomena as backdrop for teaching and learning. Examples of these things we call artifacts include, but are certainly not limited to, school calendars, master schedules, student schedules, course syllabi, teacher-made assignments, scored student work—all sources of data schools can analyze to make any updraft/downdraft forces visible.

These artifacts are valuable sources of data that let schools gain reliable information by asking serious research questions about their work, then exploring answers by way of artifact analyses. Does your high school expect all students to achieve at high levels, or do they actually create classrooms that sort students into levels on a continuum of success and failure? Do teachers teach in conditions that support their holding high expectations for all, or do the conditions of demand and support vary from period to period? In short, to what degree do your schools have updraft/down-draft dynamics interfering with the goal of success for all?

Because artifacts emerge from each school's unique set of choices, they serve as indicators of that school's core values and help us understand what, in fact, schools are really doing to create the best educational experience they can for all students. Analyzing artifacts is a strategy used by qualitative researchers, and it can be added to the high school data repertoire as yet another powerful way of viewing the work of public education through the lens of data.

It takes careful analysis for schools to look boldly beneath the obvious to identify how they may be inadvertently, or perhaps consciously, sorting students into categories that lead to—or perpetuate—social class differences. As discussed in chapters 1 and 2, for example, there are those in the current educational arena who adamantly hold to old sorting norms while others protest that the old norms block necessary opportunities and access to many students. What makes it hard sometimes to spot the old from the new is that jargon can make it sound as if the old is the new—educators are adept at "talking the talk," a far different thing than "walking the talk." Schools may offer, for example, a lot of text and talk on meeting standards in their school improvement plans. However, such talk may not pan out in reality.

Analysis of artifacts lets schools look with clear eyes at what they are doing. The information that results from these types of analyses can pave the way for more thoughtful, research-grounded conversations on secondary school reform, as well as for more innovative strategizing in making changes in the conditions that inhibit quality secondary teaching and learning.

WHY ANALYZE ARTIFACTS?

Recognizing artifacts as valuable sources of data helps schools scan the horizon for information to look more closely at the pathway that leads to results. While much of the data normally used to drive reform is focused on the end results, less data is available to help schools individually gauge the choices they are making along the way that lead to those results.

Analyses of artifacts helps schools look through the lens of data at the choices they are making on their journey toward school reform. By analyzing artifacts, schools can learn to look closely at powers under their own control, such as how they choose to use the time, talent, and energy available to them to teach students to be successful. They can look openly at their communication to parents and students by analyzing language used in course selection documents and student handbooks with information on graduation requirements. Rather than looking outward, blaming others for poor results, analyzing artifacts lets schools look for the power to succeed within their collective grasp.

Four Good Reasons

There are strong reasons for analyzing artifacts, and we will look at each in greater detail: (1) connecting research and practice, (2) accounting for use of human resources, (3) identifying conditions that support or constrain quality teaching, and (4) looking for equity and inequity in high expectations and high support.

1. Connecting Research and Practice

In chapter 2, we saw from the research the powerful impact updraft/downdraft forces can have on teachers and students as they go about their daily work of teaching and learning. By examining artifacts for equity in areas that impact teaching and learning, schools can view their culture from a fresh perspective and adopt the researcher's eye as they look within. They can learn to see the context in which high school teaching and learning occur, and to determine whether or not the context sufficiently supports teachers and students in their work.

For example, according to Murphy and Hallinger (1989, p. 131), "the most important question in the area of educational reform in general, and educational equity specifically, is what is going to be taught—to whom and by whom." Yet becoming clear about what is taught "to whom and by whom" is not automatically a part of the data that most schools analyze. By learning to inspect course selection documents and course syllabi, schools can find similarities and differences in "what" is going to be taught. By learning to scrutinize master schedules, schools can fairly easily construct data that lets them look closely at which teachers are assigned to different groups of students. Master schedule analysis, combined with background information on teacher quality (experience, degree, certification), can show whether or not there are differences in the competence levels of teachers assigned to different groups. While the research gives strong indication of what to look for, educators must use that information to look specifically in their own back yards to see if, and to what extent, they mirror the dynamics suggested by research—the good, the bad, and the ugly.

One California high school was shocked at the results that emerged from careful analysis of the master schedule they had used for years. In looking at the quality of teachers assigned to different grades, they found overwhelmingly that the veteran teachers were assigned to the upper grades, and more specifically to the Advanced Placement courses. On the other hand, teachers in the earlier high school grades were much more likely to be new teachers with fewer credentials. When they combined this information with their dropout rates and identified the grade in which most students left school (end of ninth grade), they could see that students most likely to be at risk were taught by the least skilled teachers. While they were aware of this information all along at some level, seeing it blatantly converted to data waved a red flag, and they could no longer ignore this reality, particularly in light of their low achievement scores and high dropout rates. Made visible by data analysis, this updraft/downdraft dynamic screamed for attention and got it.

2. Accounting for Use of Human Resources

Even though personnel costs are the major expenditure of schools, it is very difficult to track how staffs' time, talent, and energy are "spent" in the economy of staff utilization. At district levels, it is not unusual to find over three-fourths of the budget spent on personnel, and often the percentages are even higher in school level budgets because the district controls many non-personnel expenditure decisions such as transportation, food services, and utilities, for example.

There are a number of checks and balances on the actual expenditure of money at both district and school levels—purchase order systems, fiscal regulations at state and district levels, and regular audits conducted by layers of professionals. There are strong systems in place for establishing salaries and benefits for paying personnel. Yet there are very loose and very few ways of monitoring how personnel, once hired, are actually used throughout the day, the month, and the year. Thus in most educational systems the vast part of the budget is spent without a strong system of analysis and accountability because there is no uniform way of tracking, analyzing, and reporting how personnel are used.

When one high school began to think about using certified staff as an economy, they found that their total certified personnel budget of just over $10 million was about 95 percent of their available "funds," while their operating and instructional budget ($533,375) was less than 5 percent of their total resources. The budget involving cash expenditures was tightly regulated by the district, but the largest proportion of the budget —personnel time—was left unfettered to school level decision-making, the only oversight an annual meeting with the superintendent to "eyeball" the master schedule.

By developing a system for analyzing how teachers and staff are used in relation to the strategic plan of the school, educators and their publics can learn to see how staff time aligns with high achievement for all—How are we using our human resources? Are leaders harnessing the power of staff time, talent, and energy with equity? Are we using people to the fullest advantage for student learning, or are they disproportionately working on non-instructional tasks? When this high school actually continued their master schedule analysis, merging information from the school budget mentioned above with the time teachers actually taught, they found that a one-minute decision on the master schedule cost them over $27,000 in personnel costs per year. Thus about 20 minutes of decision in regard to how staff would be used across the year pretty much equaled their overall operating budget. By developing ways the school could see how important each decision was, they could begin to understand the actual economy of their school and to make decisions with greater awareness. When dollar figures were added for specific teachers, they could also see that more money per student was spent on upper grade, advanced students than was spent on students most at risk in lower grades.

3. Identifying Conditions that Support or Constrain Quality Teaching

Research shows that teachers are most likely to engage in the hard work of teaching when they believe that teaching is both important and possible. The conditions in which teaching occurs have tremendous power to constrain or support effective teaching, yet these conditions are often unexamined and leaders are often unaware of their existence. There is tendency to focus directly on teacher training and professional development, all necessary and positive, without recognizing that there are conditions of teaching that either support or inhibit effective work performance. In some cases, teachers know much more than the conditions allow them to use, while in others they may need new skills.

How can schools recognize the various pressures they are putting on their teachers to see the extent to which teachers operate in an updraft or a downdraft—or both? How can schools adopt the classroom teacher view to see if the system supports them in holding high expectations for all, or if they have to fight the system to both demand and support students in achieving high expectations with consistency? Are some teachers supported in holding high expectations while others are not? Are the same teachers supported differently in holding high expectations, depending on differences in courses they are teaching or students they are serving? Taking a hard look at artifacts can give insight into these critical questions.

Much of this kind of thinking shows up in the emphasis on personalization of the high school, supporting the movement toward Small Learning Communities in which teachers must know fewer students as learners and as individuals for longer periods of time than has been tradition in the comprehensive high school. It also shows up in discussions on block scheduling, in which teachers teach fewer total students. Both have strong impacts on what we call "teacher load," the sheer numbers of students that teachers must know and be able to teach on a regular basis.

For example, if a teacher has huge numbers of total students in their classes on a daily basis, that teacher has many constraints that tend to limit effective teaching. If a teacher has 150 students per day (5 classes of 30 students each), he or she must spend 12.5 hours solid in order to grade and give student feedback—an assignment that takes 5 minutes of their time per paper. One high school found that teachers in high track classes had an average of 80 students per day because of smaller class sizes, while general track teachers had almost double that number. With impossible scoring times, teachers are highly unlikely to give complex assignments that require thoughtful scoring. Thus teachers placed in different tracks faced very different dynamics in holding high expectations, with teachers in the higher tracks operating in a contextual updraft while lower track teachers taught in downdraft conditions.

Further analysis, from a slightly different viewpoint, might show that teaching well may be virtually impossible because of time limitations. Do teachers have enough time to teach standards? Do students have enough time to learn standards? For example, if a teacher has 180 calendar days of 48-minute classes, he or she actually has only about 18 eight-hour days to teach one subject, assuming no interruptions. With fire drills, assemblies, snow days, and the lost time of settling into class as well as gathering books to leave, it is easy to lose 10 percent or more of the available time, which gives teachers only 16 eight-hour days. For some students, those in the updraft, this may be enough, particularly if the teacher is able to extend learning time with quality homework assignments. For students who are behind in basic skills or who struggle to learn, however, this time may be a pittance. Analysis of graduation requirements might show that teachers are able to double or triple time for students who are behind, or it might show that they are locked into the small amount of time given because of the high number of required courses.

Yet another view, the analysis of the student's schedule can give other valuable data in measuring why school is working—or not—to produce success. An analysis of a middle years student's schedule in England, for example, showed that there were conflicting policies at the national level. Course requirements demanded a wide-reaching array of courses, and analysis of a typical student schedule showed a five-day cycle of courses taught by almost twenty different teachers in order to meet those course requirements. Yet the end of middle years exam, called Key Stage Three exam, focused tightly on only a few curriculum areas: reading, writing, math, and science. It soon became crystal clear, thanks to a student named Patrick Henry, that student time for learning was actually very tightly aligned with the content exams taken at age 16, rather than with the much more narrow spectrum of the age 13 exam. Thus, there was limited time to prepare for this Key Stage Three exam. Plans to hold teachers accountable and to provide intensive professional development were not enough to create updraft for all unless disconnects in alignment between goals and time were resolved.

4. Looking for Equity and Inequity in High Expectations and High Support

The overarching theme that undergirds all these conversations, from the research sketch in chapter 2 to the more immediate list of implications, is this: is there equity in your school? Do teachers have equitable opportunity to teach, and do students have equitable opportunity to learn? Using this dominant theme, schools can ask critical research questions and look to artifacts for answers.

For example, schools might ask questions about holding high expectations for all such as: what are we doing as a school to contribute to high secondary student achievement? Are we actually, without meaning to, pressing for low achievement for some and high achievement for others? Or do we hold high expectations for all?

By analyzing syllabi for courses with similar titles yet in different tracks, schools could find vast differences in the amount of content covered as well as the depth and level of rigor expected for successful course completion. Or by analyzing graduation expectations and student transcripts, schools might find huge inequities in the level of rigor that varies with gender, race or ethnicity, or differences in end points such as pre-vocational versus pre-college preparatory programs.

CONCLUSION

Learning to analyze artifacts as a rich source of data adds a new lens to high school reform and gives schools and their publics many new tools for improvement.

It takes careful thinking by administrators and teachers to look at all the ready sources of available information beyond what we usually think of when we consider data in our schools. Most importantly, it takes a willingness to see and talk about the updraft/downdraft forces that have created an uneven, differently delivered educational world inside the high school. One could imagine this process of uncovering the meaning hidden inside artifacts as one of discovery. Just as archeologists and anthropologists work, school communities can also uncover meanings within their buildings.

By making these areas of importance identified by researchers visible, schools can then be prepared to make informed choices as they change contexts for teaching and learning—contexts that tend to differentiate expectations rather than to support high achievement expectations for all students. Only then can schools correct or create new conditions and infrastructures necessary to deliver equity and excellence in education to all students.

In the next chapter, we visit a single high school to see how it used artifacts to analyze time available for learning and teaching to better view the context in which teachers teach and learners learn.

4

A High School Case Study

You've got to consider return on investment, and the biggest investment is time.

—Ollie Jones 2001

We know that teachers are put in situations that dampen their capacity.

—Jan Sommerville 2001

Welcome to Rockdale High, home of 132 teachers and 2,650 students who teach and learn together daily in the heart of the city. This chapter is a simulation case study designed to show some of the ways artifact analysis can be used to construct data, as well as to show updraft/downdraft dynamics that provide context in support of quality teaching and learning, or that silently constrain both.

Serving a zone that ranges from families of classic wealth to those barely surviving bone-grinding poverty, the Rockdale High School student body is highly diverse. According to last year's state report on demographics, about 39 percent of the students are Latino (mostly from Mexico); 32 percent are African American; 23 percent are white; 5 percent are Asian Pacific Islander, and 1 percent are "other." Only 68 percent of the students qualify for free and reduced lunch, an amount that falls barely, and tantalizingly, short of meeting the district's Title One requirements. For the most part, white students dominate the wealthier student groups, while students of color are over-represented in the poorer student groups. Historically, both the white and African American populations have been established in the neighborhood for many years, while the

39

Latino families have arrived over the past 30 years to work in local industry.

The high school struggles to keep students in school, both to hold the wealthier students who tend to waffle between public and private school choices as well as the poor who leave in waves throughout the year and never complete school. Thus far, with an intensive district-lead mandate for reform, the school has been able to hold the wealthier students, although their grasp is never fully secure. Little has been done to quell the dropout rate, and high school students leave in droves, drawn by the call of a strong local economy struggling to find adequate supplies of labor.

Here we offer district and school administrators, teachers, school boards and community members a case study to show how artifacts analysis was used to see how equitable secondary students' experiences were in one high school. This case study on the analysis of artifacts offers a practical view of processes for looking at practices inside individual schools. It is an example, and certainly is not exhaustive. The processes that emerge, both in this case study as well as in this book, offer schools a way to research their own sites and to draw conclusions about how students are, or are not receiving the instruction, supports and conditions necessary to become college-ready. These tools are not new nor are they special instruments: most are readily available and may even be on our desks. Yet, they tell us a lot about whether we are delivering a rigorous education to all students; one that prepares them for future academic studies, for college and for the high-performance workplace.

Come on in!

ROCKDALE HIGH SCHOOL

Lockers crammed full of coats, books, old papers, and treasures unknown greet visitors as they walk into the front lobby of the classic old 1930s high school. Worn marble steps hint of students long gone, retirees basking in tropical sun, while grimy remnants of the melting week-old snowstorm greet today's students and staff. Rockdale High offers the full range of programs familiar in most comprehensive high schools, a vast array of courses reflecting decades of policy decisions. Several years ago, the district undertook a significant high school reform based on the idea of the Certificate of Mastery, with students required to demonstrate proficiency on standards via a series of portfolio entries. While the Certificate of Mastery idea was created to focus the high school experience on academic proficiency in basics, the district missed that point. They created performance measures for long lists of district standards that must be met in order for students to be promoted to grade 11.

Under the Certificate of Mastery design, students and teachers are separated onto different floors, thus dividing the 9–10 program and the 11–12 program into two very separate learning communities. In grades 9 and 10, teams of teachers teach students a common core curriculum with the exception of the Preparatory Advanced Scholars Program (PASP) for students who excel. These PASP ninth- and tenth-graders are taught on a separate team using a more advanced curriculum. When students reach grades 11 and 12, they have a choice to make among four major paths to graduation: Advanced Scholars Program, College Prep, Tech Prep, and Workforce Prep. *The Rockdale High Curriculum Guide* welcomes students to these four choices as follows:

- The goal of the Advanced Scholars Program is to prepare students for entry into elite postsecondary schools and success at the graduate level in professional programs.
- The goal of the College Prep program is to prepare students for entry and success in two and four year colleges.
- The goal of the Tech Prep program is to prepare students for entry and success in postsecondary vocational-technical programs.
- The goal of the Workforce Prep program is to prepare students for entry into the workplace upon graduation from high school.

While the goals of reform were noble, the results have been disappointing. State assessments indicate that only 2.5 out of 10 students are proficient in the areas of reading and mathematics at grade 11, results that have been unfortunately stable for the past fifteen years. The performance portfolio

Layered Society

"The way I see it, you just ought to keep the top third, the cream, to go to college. The middle third-they go to technical school. You know, the ones that can be good carpenters. And the bottom third—you save them for pulling up the net." (teacher in Gulf Coast shrimping village)

system designed at the policy level to indicate proficiency in standards became, in practice, a checklist system for tracking assignments completed in related areas. Despite good intentions, the standards-based system was never really brought to life in the district.

In order to look more closely at the path that lead to these stubbornly disappointing results, the newly hired superintendent chose to conduct an audit using selected artifacts—an analysis of the district calendar to establish the total amount of available time for teaching and learning, a comparison of use of teacher time and teaching load using the master schedule, and a comparison of the use of student time using sample student schedules—to offer fresh perspective. By asking the following questions, the district hoped to find insight into the challenges staff and students face in achieving success for all: (1) How much time is available for teaching and learning in a calendar year? (2) Does Rockdale High support teachers in teaching students to achieve, or are there updraft/downdraft dynamics that press teacher to sort students? (3) Does Rockdale High use time to support all students in learning, or are there updraft/downdraft dynamics that tend to sort students into some who succeed, others who fail?

The results were astounding. In the following three sections, we take a closer look at answers the district found from artifact analyses using these three critical questions to guide their research.

HOW MUCH TIME IS AVAILABLE FOR TEACHING AND LEARNING IN A CALENDAR YEAR?

If we are to fully understand the conditions under which teachers and students work, we must analyze how time is used to support or constrain effective learning and teaching. District calendars reveal the first round of information about how districts and schools are managing time and to what extent a district can deliver on its promise to educate all students. In this calendar-analysis section, we use actual data provided by Bill Kiefer of the School District of Lancaster in Lancaster, Pennsylvania, including the use of his templates.

In order to analyze the Rockdale District calendar, Kiefer first collected and organized information. He got copies of the school calendar and found out the total number of days in the teachers' calendars, the total number of days teachers actually teach students, and the total number of days of vacation time or other such days. Because the school calendar was simply a list of dates, he got a regular monthly calendar so he could physically see the teaching and non-teaching time available in each school year. He then marked each teaching day, vacation day, professional development day, early release day, and other categories on the monthly calendar. In the end, he constructed a month-by-month picture of the time available for teaching.

The following calendar slides (figures 4.1 through 4.5) show the results. The data do not include other smaller sources of lost time, such as fire drills, recess, passing time, etc., although it is certainly possible to calculate available time to that level of detail.

When you analyze these separate slides, you will see this calendar reveals that students are actually involved in instructional class time a total of 152 days possible days. In terms of the school year, this means that students spend 82 percent of a 185-day school year inside schools in academic work. If you put this in terms of a 365-day calendar year, students are in instruction only 42 percent of the year. Calculated without weekends, students on this calendar spend 152 days out of 261 days a year, or about 31 weeks out of 52 weeks a year or 58 percent of the year.

This breakdown analysis reveals that time on task is a precious commodity within the school year as well as during class time. If all students are to have time to master complex material and subject matter, then more time needs to be built in to accommodate students' varying pace and needs for opportunities to practice new skills and learn unfamiliar material. It suggests that this district and its schools need to set priorities based on other data and on student achievement data.

DOES ROCKDALE HIGH SUPPORT TEACHERS
IN TEACHING ALL STUDENTS TO ACHIEVE?

The master schedule is a rich source of answers to the question, "Are we using staff time wisely in supporting both quality teaching as well as high level students achievement?" There are two major areas we considered in looking at sections taken from the sample master schedule: (1) the impact of differences in number of periods taught in the 9–10 and 11–12 pro-

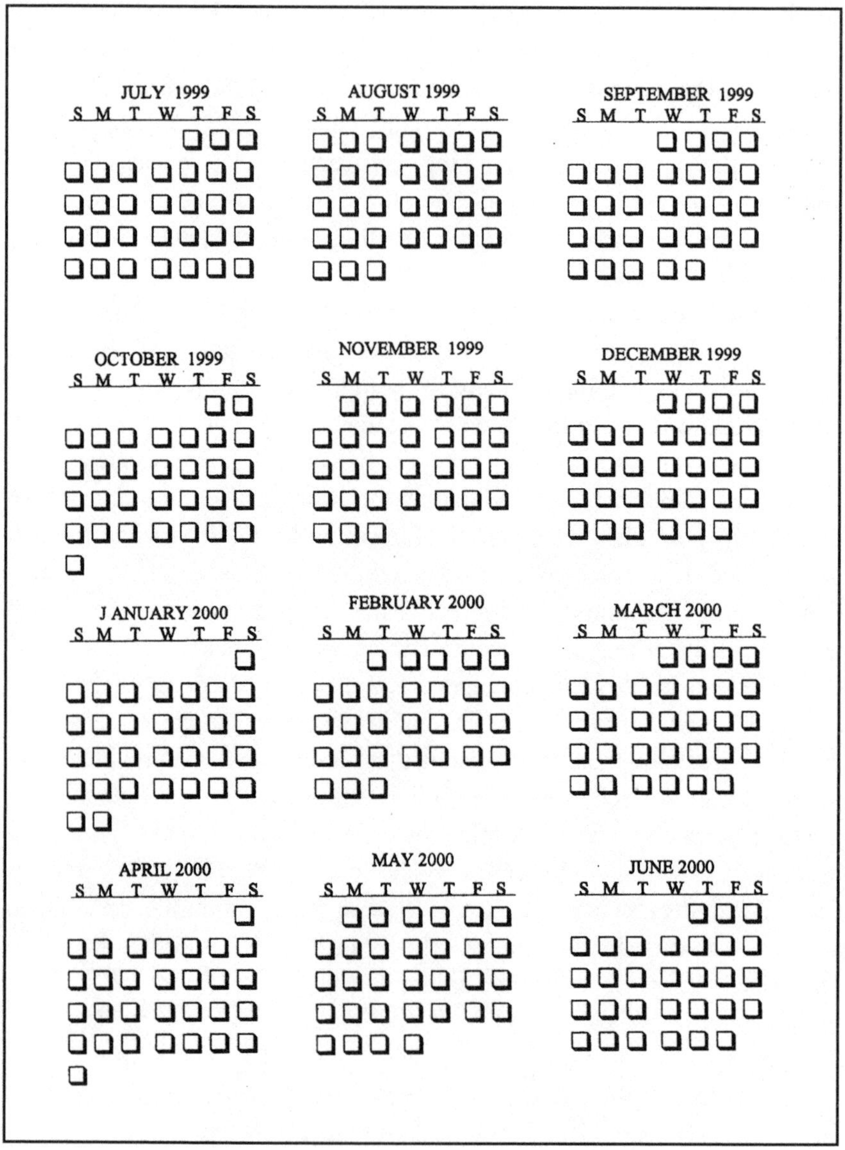

Chapter 4

JULY 1999
S M T W T F S
□□□
□□□ □□□□
□□□ □□□□
□□□ □□□□
□□□ □□□□

AUGUST 1999
S M T W T F S
□□□ □□□□
□□□ □□□□
□□□ □□□□
□□□ □□□□
□□□

SEPTEMBER 1999
S M T W T F S
□□□□
□□□ □□□□
□□□ □□□□
□□□ □□□□
□□□ □□

OCTOBER 1999
S M T W T F S
□□
□□□ □□□□
□□□ □□□□
□□□ □□□□
□□□ □□□□
□

NOVEMBER 1999
S M T W T F S
□□ □ □□□
□□□ □ □□□
□□□ □ □□□
□□□

DECEMBER 1999
S M T W T F S
□□□□
□□□ □□□□
□□□ □□□□
□□□ □□□

JANUARY 2000
S M T W T F S
□
□□□ □□□□
□□□ □□□□
□□□ □□□□
□□□ □□□□
□□

FEBRUARY 2000
S M T W T F S
□ □□ □□
□□□ □□ □□
□□□ □□ □□
□□□

MARCH 2000
S M T W T F S
□□□□
□□ □□□□□
□□ □□□□□
□□ □□□□

APRIL 2000
S M T W T F S
□
□□ □□□□□
□□□ □□□□
□□□ □□□□
□□□ □□□□
□

MAY 2000
S M T W T F S
□□ □□ □□
□□□ □□ □□
□□□ □□ □□
□□□ □

JUNE 2000
S M T W T F S
□□□
□□□ □□□□
□□□ □□□□
□□□ □□□□
□□□ □□□

Figure 4.1
The full-year calendar

(Source: School District of Lancaster)

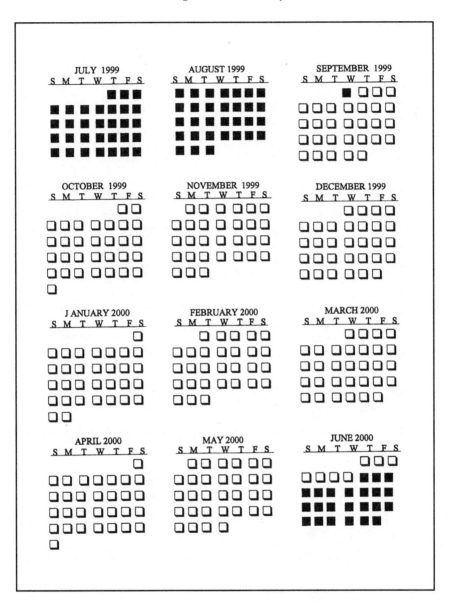

Figure 4.2
Less summer vacation

(Source: School District of Lancaster)

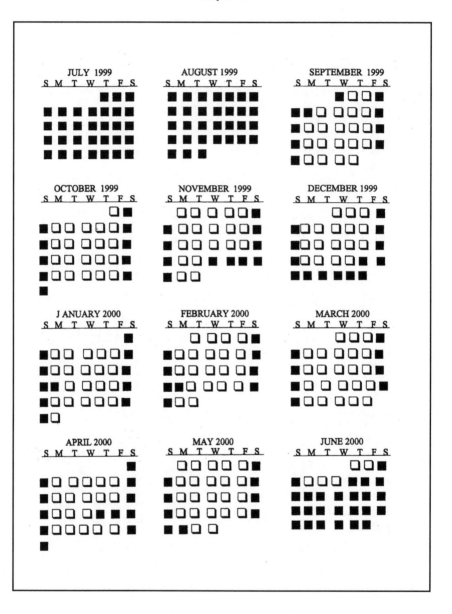

Figure 4.3
Less weekends and holidays

(Source: School District of Lancaster)

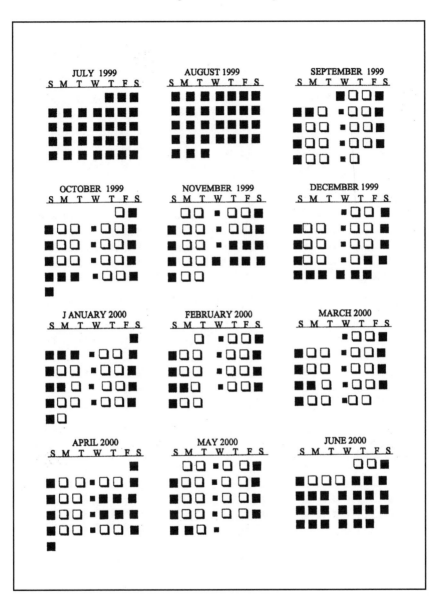

Figure 4.4
Less professional development days and
early dismissal/parent conferences

(Source: School District of Lancaster)

Chapter 4

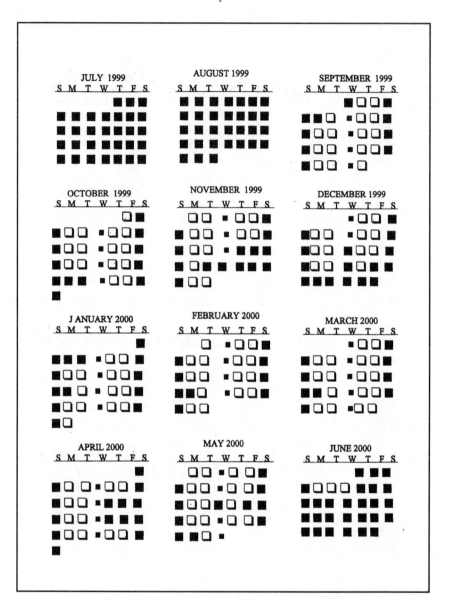

Figure 4.5
*Less class picnic, class trip, Thanksgiving feast, Christmas,
Kwanzaa, Hanukkah celebration, awards, assemblies, concerts*

(Source: School District of Lancaster)

grams and (2) the scoring time impact of different teacher-student loads on teacher time. This is merely an example to kick off your own thinking as you convert your master schedule to data capable of being analyzed to see if students have equal opportunity to learn, and teachers have support for holding high expectations and moving students to high performance.

Before we begin to take a look at these two areas, we first invite you to look at samples from the master schedule that was analyzed.

SAMPLE MASTER SCHEDULE ARTIFACTS

For this analysis we selected representative teacher assignments for each track offered. Before we begin the discussion of what we found, take a look at the following samples (figures 4.6 through 4.10) from the Rockdale High School master schedule.

When we analyzed these separate slides, we found a number of inequities that impacted teacher ability to hold high expectations for all.

Subject	Period 1	Period 2	Period 3	Period 4	Period 5	Period 6	Period 7	Period 8	Total Students
Comm. Arts	Prep	CA 22	CA 29	CA 26	Lunch/ SSR	CA 24	CA 28	CA 25	154
Social Studies	SS 25	SS 25	SS 27	SS 23	Lunch/SSR	SS 27	SS 27	Prep	154
Science	Science 27	Prep	Science 26	Science 29	Lunch/SSR	Science 19	Science 26	Science 27	154
Math	Math 25	Math 23	Math 26	Math 27	Lunch/SSR	Math 28	Prep	Math 27	154
World Language	WLang 21	WLang 27	WLang 25	WLang 24	Lunch/SSR	Prep	WLang 28	WLang 29	154

Figure 4.6
Regular Team Sample

Chapter 4

Subject	Period 1	Period 2	Period 3	Period 4	Period 5	Period 6	Period 7	Period 8	Total Students
Comm. Arts	Prep	Pre-CA **9**	CA **21**	Pre-CA **25**	CA **17**	Lunch/SSR	CA **14**	Pre-CA **26**	**112**
Social Studies	SS **15**	SS **21**	SS **14**	Pre-Am History **24**	Pre-Am History **12**	Lunch/SSR	Prep	Pre-Euro History **26**	**112**
Science	Pre-Sci **7**	Prep	Pre-Sci **27**	Science **21**	Pre-Sci **26**	Lunch/SSR	Sci **15**	Sci **14**	**110**
Math	Math **13**	Math **13**	Pre-Math **26**	Pre-Math **14**	Prep	Lunch/SSR	Pre-Math **19**	Math **22**	**111**
World Language	French **15**	Spanish **8**	Spanish **20**	Prep	Pre-French **22**	Lunch/SSR	Pre-Sp **32**	Spanish **25**	**122**

Figure 4.7
Preparatory Advanced Scholars Program Team Sample

Subject	Period 1	Period 2	Period 3	Period 4	Period 5	Period 6	Period 7	Period 8	Total Students
C Arts	English Lit **16**	Prep	AP Lang & Comp **20**	General CA **32**	General CA **24**	Lunch	General CA **26**	General CA **26**	**144**
Math	Prep	Study Hall 23,16,25,29,24	Gen Math **17**	Gen Math **30**	Lunch	Gen Math **19**	Gen Math **31**	Gen Math **29**	**126+**
Social Studies	World Cult (Team 10) **30**	Prep	World Cult (Team 10) **28**	World Cult (Team 10) **31**	Law & Ethics **17**	Lunch	Const Law **19**	Study 16,26,18,15,19	**125 +**
Math	Prep	Alg 2 **33**	Alg 2 **32**	Lunch	Gen Math **30**	Alg 2 **12**	Gen Math **31**	Study 14,23,18,14,18	**138+**
Science	Prep	Applied Science **28**	Study 15,15,13,18,16	Biology (Team 10) **30**	Lunch	Physics **15**	Physics **27**	Physics **27**	**127+**

Figure 4.8
Regular Teacher Sample

Subject	Period 1	Period 2	Period 3	Period 4	Period 5	Period 6	Period 7	Period 8	Total Students
Graphic Comm	Graph C I 18	Graph C I 18	Graph C I 18	Lunch	Prep	Graph C 2 7	Graph C 2 7	Graph C 2 7	25/75 eq
Cadd	Cadd I 11	Cadd I 11	Cadd I 11	Prep	Lunch	Cadd I 9 / Cadd 2 6	Cadd I 9 / Cadd 2 6	Cadd I 9 / Cadd 2 6	26/79 eq
C Arts	CA 30	Study 26,17, 13,30, 21	Tech Writ 22	ATC1 BA 31	Tech Write 29	Lunch	Prep	ATC1 BA/BM 28	132
Science	Study 14,18,17,19,17	Astronomy 25	App Sci 20	App Sci 26	App Sci 26	Lunch	App Sci 26	Prep	123

Figure 4.9
Vocational Teacher Sample

Subject	Period 1	Period 2	Period 3	Period 4	Period 5	Period 6	Period 7	Period 8	Total Students
Computer Science	Pre-IB 13 / Visual Basic 1 19	Pre-IB 19	AP/IB CS 19	AP Statistics	Prep	Lunch	AP/IB CS 18	AP CS 3	73
Science	Prep	IB Chem 2 9	Pre-IB Chem 26	Lunch	Pre-IB Chem 25	AP Chem 16	IB Chem 10	Pre-IB Chem 20	106
IB Coord	IB Coord 0	IB Coord 0	IB Coord 0	Appl Psych Soc 15	Theory of Kn 1 11	Lunch	Prep	IB Coord 0	26
Social Studies	Study 14,19,16 / SAP M,W	AP Art Hist 22	AP M AM Hist 15	AP Am Hist 27	Lunch	Prep	IB HOA-HL 5	AP M Am Hist 18	87
W Lang	Prep	Pre-IB AP Spanish 14	Spanish 4 14	Lunch	IB/AP Sp 4 14	Pre-IB/AP Sp 22	IB/AP Sp 4 12	IB/AP Sp 5 12	88

Figure 4.10
Advanced Scholars Program Teacher Sample
11-12 International Baccalaureate Program/
Advanced Placement Teacher Sample

Time for Teaching

Number of Periods Taught

First, we will look at use of teacher time for teaching. Let's examine the relative amount of time teachers spend teaching, starting with the number of periods teachers teach out of an eight-period day. In the 9–10 program, the teachers teach 6 out of 8 periods per day, the contractual limit for full-time secondary teaching. In the 11–12 program, on the other hand, teachers teach 5 of 8 periods per day, less than the full contract requires. There are 66 teachers in each of the programs, a total of 132 teachers in all.

Let's look at these figures in a slightly different way, beginning to treat this information available through the master schedule artifact as data. If 66 teachers teach 6 periods per day, there are a total of 396 class periods taught per day in the 9–10 program. If 66 teachers in the 11–12 program teach 5 periods per day, there are a total of 330 class periods taught per day—66 fewer periods than in the 9–10 program. If there are 66 fewer periods taught, how many equivalent FTEs are lost in the 11–12 program? Because one full-time teacher teaches 6 periods, a total of 11 full-time teacher equivalents (66 periods/6 periods per full-time teacher) are lost when 66 teachers are unassigned for one possible teaching period each.

Length of Lunch Period

Next, let's take a look at the impact of time spent in lunch. Students and teachers in the 9–10 program have 30 minutes for lunch, while students and teachers spend a full 48 minute period eating lunch in the 11–12 program. When a full-time teacher teaches 6 periods (48 minutes each), they have 288 minutes of teaching time per day. Thinking collectively, if 66 teachers spend 18 extra minutes at lunch, the cost in total time is 1,188 teacher-minutes per day total. If one full-time teacher can teach 288 minutes per day, the relative full-time teacher equivalence lost for 1,188 total additional lunchtime minutes spent is slightly over 4 teachers.

Combined Impact

What is the combined impact of 5 rather than 6 teaching periods in combination with a longer lunch period? With a total of 11 full time-teacher equivalents lost because of teaching 5 rather than 6 periods, and over 4 teacher equivalents lost because of extending lunch 18 minutes, there is a functional total of slightly over 15 full time teacher equivalents lost at the 11–12 program.

In addition to thinking of this impact in terms of full-time teaching equivalents, we can think of the fiscal impact of these two decisions. In this district, the average teacher salary with benefits is $57, 500. If over 15 full-time teaching equivalents are lost, the cost exceeds $862,500, a figure greater than the annual total materials and supply budgets of both programs combined.

While there might be palatable reasons for making these choices, the key dynamic in terms of updraft/downdraft thinking is that the teachers in the 9–10 program are disadvantaged in holding high expectations, while the teachers in the 11–12 program are advantaged on this one view of the data. However, it is possible that there are other variables that might somewhat offset this advantage, such as each teacher's total student load. If teachers in the 11–12 program have larger classes, for example, both sets of faculty would be teaching equal numbers of students.

Teacher-Student Load

In analyzing the teacher-student load, we looked at two key factors: (1) the assignment of staff to grades 9–10 and grades 11–12 in relation to the numbers of students in those grades and (2) teacher scoring time for the total number of students taught.

Student-Teacher Ratio

First, we look at the assignment of staff to campuses in relation to the assignment of students to campuses to see if it is proportional or not. For example, let's take a look at assignments of staff to each program in relation to total numbers of students served:

- *9–10 Program:* In the 9–10 program, there are 46 core teachers and 20 non-core teachers, for a total of 66 teachers. There are a total of 1,296 students, and if evenly divided among the 66 teachers, the student-teacher ratio would be 19.6:1.

- *11–12 Program:* In the 9–10 program, there are 37 core teachers and 29 non-core teachers, for a total of 66 teachers. There are a total of 1,023 students, and if evenly divided among the 66 teachers, the student-teacher ratio is 15.5:1.

Obviously, the 11–12 program is significantly greater resourced, with an overall student-teacher ratio in the 9–10 program just over 4 students greater per teacher than would be found in the 11–12 program. Although we did not explore this difference further, it would be a logical next step to look at this artifact data in combination with the school's dropout data as well as discipline data to see the impact of differences in the two student bodies, since many of the more challenged and challenging students tend to be gone from high school by the upper grades.

Total Student Load

Next, we compare the relative numbers of total teacher-student contacts—the total number of students teachers must know as learners and teach—from one teacher to the next, from one program to the next. In the representative sample master schedule selected, teachers in the regular track 9–10 core subjects team have an average of 154 total student contacts per day, while high track teacher numbers range from 110 to 122 students per day. Teachers in the regular track 11–12 courses have daily contact numbers ranging from 125 to 144. Teachers in 11–12 vocational lab courses see a total of 25 to 26 students per day, for three-period blocks, while vocational core course teachers (communication arts, math, and so forth) serve from 123 to 132 students per day. In the Advanced Scholars Program classes in grades 11 and 12, student contact loads for teachers range from 26 for the part-time coordinator to 106 students per day.

When you look at the different loads on the two campuses, the first question to arise is "Why do 9–10 teachers carry a higher load?" In this case, most of the advanced courses and lab courses are held on the 11–12 campus with lower class size numbers. One way to interpret this is that the general classes have more students in order to accommodate AP, IB and other advanced courses as well as lab courses, such as graphics and business technology. Another way to look at this is that the bulk of the student body is sandwiched between two sections, one college-bound and one vocational-oriented. General education teachers carry about 150 students a day, while advanced and lab course teachers have significantly less than that number, with some advanced classes having as few as five in a class. This may well create conditions for teaching that are more difficult for the largest number of students and their teachers.

Whatever the reason, these differences have tremendous impact on the context in which students and teachers work. Think, for example of the impact on the teacher when scoring student work. If a teacher has to score papers from 154 students, spending only 5 minutes per paper, their total scoring time is 770 minutes, or 12.8 hours. On the other hand, the teacher who has to score 87 papers spends 435 minutes, or 7.3 hours in scoring time—a difference of 5.5 hours. This is a conservative estimate of teacher time, since most written work of substance takes more than 5 minutes per paper, and these figures assume constant work without break. Think, furthermore, of the impact of these different ratios on opportunity to know students well as learners, and to personalize their educational experiences.

In short, it is clear that context limits or supports a teacher's ability to hold high expectations and provide appropriate supports so students can achieve those expectations. It is also clear that there is inequality both between tracks and levels in terms of the teacher's ability to teach well, and thus, updraft/downdraft dynamics are actively pressing on teachers differently in this school. Teachers in the 11–12 program have more time, smaller class sizes, and fewer total students with considerably less scoring time. And teachers in the high-status Advanced Scholars Program classes are resourced better than other programs, both at 9–10 as well as 11–12 levels. Of course, you will have to look closer in order to understand the nuances of a master schedule analysis. There are certainly other duties that have to be performed in a high school. In this case, however, the differences are clearly categorical, and the upper grades are advantaged while the lower grades are not. Since this school has a particularly high dropout rate and the number of difficult-to-serve students is reduced at the upper grades, the impact of inequities in time load, as well as teacher-student load discussed earlier, are magnified.

DOES ROCKDALE HIGH USE TIME TO
SUPPORT STUDENTS IN LEARNING?

While the master schedule offers insight into the world of teaching, student schedules offer yet another view of the school using the student's lens to view the world of learning. In this analysis, we will look in particular at use of time within context of the student day.

Sample Student Schedules

For purposes of this exercise, we will concentrate solely on differences in general track schedules in the 9–10 program versus general track students in the 11–12 program. We use sample student schedules from each.

Analysis of Student Schedules

Let's take a look at the differences in basic student schedules between the 9–10 program and the 11–12 program, with both programs having a total of 434 available minutes, or 7.23 hours per day.

In the 9–10 program, students spend 85 minutes in total non-course time: homeroom is 10 minutes; passing time (9 moves @ 5 minutes each) is 45 minutes; and lunch is 30 minutes. The remaining time, 349 minutes, is spent in class. Without including lost time for settling into class and getting ready to leave, students in the 9–10 program spend 19.6 percent of their available time in non-course time and 80.4 percent of their possible time in class.

Furthermore, look at the number of different courses and teachers that students must know and adjust to because of the rotation in special courses such as art, music, and PE. Assuming that students move to new teachers for each subject because of certification and assuming that homeroom and SSR are leading one of these teachers, students must work under the different styles and expectations of 11 different teachers during the school year.

At the 11–12 program, students spend 98 minutes in total non-course time: homeroom is 10 minutes; passing time (8 moves @ 5 minutes each) is 40 minutes, and lunch is 48 minutes. The remaining time, 336 minutes,

Student Schedule 1

General Track 9–10 Student Schedule with 30-Minute Lunch

HR	Homeroom	10 Minutes
1	Communication Arts	48 Minutes
2	Math	48 Minutes
3	Science	48 Minutes
4	Social Studies	48 Minutes
5	Lunch/SSR	30/18 Minutes
6	World Language	48 Minutes
7	Art/Music	48 Minutes (change at semester)
8	PE/FCS/Tech Ed/Computer	48 Minutes (change at 9 weeks)

Student Schedule 2

General Track 11–12 Student Schedule with 48-Minute Lunch

HR	Homeroom	10 Minutes
1	Communication Arts	48 Minutes
2	Math	48 Minutes
3	Science	48 Minutes
4	Social Studies	48 Minutes
5	Lunch	48 Minutes
6	World Language	48 Minutes
7	Elective	48 Minutes
8	Study Hall	48 Minutes

is spent in class. Without including lost time for settling into class and getting ready to leave, students in the 11–12 program spend 22.6 percent of their available time in non-course time and 77.4 percent of their possible time in class.

Furthermore, look at the number of different courses and teachers that students must know and adjust to in comparison with the 9–10 students. Assuming that students move to new teachers for each subject because of certification and that homeroom and study hall is not a teaching period, they must work under the different styles and expectations of only 6 different teachers during the school year—5 teachers less than 9–10 students.

LESSONS LEARNED AT ROCKDALE HIGH

So what did Rockdale High learn from their artifacts analysis? First and foremost, they learned that there was not equality or equity for teaching and learning. For teachers and students in the Advanced Scholars Program, learning and teaching was supported by strong allocation of teacher resources. On the other hand, for students and teachers in the general track, time was in much shorter supply.

Before using artifacts to look at the context in which teaching and learning were occurring, leaders assumed that teacher training through professional development and accountability pressures would be the key strategies for school improvement. While those arenas continued to have the same strong emphasis after analysis, administration could clearly see the confounding effects of a context that failed to support teachers and learners. For example, if teachers do not have enough time to teach, nor learners to learn, all the professional development and teacher talent in the world will not be enough. On the other hand, if teachers and students simply increase time without changing practice, as we will discuss in chapter 6, schools will continue to be unsuccessful.

The following year, the school took action and equalized numbers so class sizes were more even across campuses and programs. By rethinking how each staff member was used, the school re-allocated some duties and found enough personnel time to create a weekly professional development program during the school day by using non-teaching time equally for all teachers. In long term, they brought in new leadership and implemented

Small Learning Communities beginning with grade 9 to increase personalization. With the number of high school requirements driving the schedule, however, they still struggle with teachers' total student contacts and scoring time across all programs.

NEXT STEPS

Now that you have an idea of what artifact analysis might look like, we move on to show some techniques for conducting artifact analysis in your own schools. In the next chapter, we offer strategies for analyzing the time context of teaching and learning—Analyzing Calendars, Student Schedules, and Master Schedules—to look for updraft/downdraft dynamics that may be sending silent messages to students, parents, and staff.

5

Analyzing Calendars, Student Schedules, and Master Schedules

A school's master schedule, for example, has many stories to tell about the distribution of curricular offerings, the distribution of teacher talent, and about a school's efficiency in using available time and human resources.

—Kati Haycock 2001

Here we offer district and school administrators, teachers, school boards and community members a set of activities to discover just how equitable secondary students' experiences are in their middle and high schools. This section on the analysis of artifacts offers examples of processes for looking at practices inside individual schools. It is an initial list, and certainly is not exhaustive. These processes offer schools a way to research their own sites and to draw conclusions about how students are or are not receiving the instruction, supports and conditions necessary to become college-ready. These tools are not new or special instruments. Most are readily available and may even be on our desks. Yet, they tell us a lot about whether we are delivering a rigorous education to all students, one that prepares them for future academic studies, for college and for the high-performance workplace.

The process of analyzing artifacts is very simple—simply repeat the following steps for each type of artifact you might choose to examine: (1) Collect and organize information; (2) Analyze the data by asking tough questions and looking critically at what you find; (3) Apply what you have learned to decision-making to create updraft for all students. We will walk you through the process for three separate types of artifacts in order to ground you in this way of thinking. Then, once you get the hang of it, you can take off into new areas of analysis as you discover more and more sources of powerful data at your fingertips.

In every instance, the secret to having usable and useful data is to be blatantly honest in looking at your school through this analytical lens. Let the information emerge without shaping it—simply record what is, and then ask tough questions about what you see. View your own school through the lens of your artifacts with a critical eye. Once you are satisfied that you have exhausted your exploration and analysis, present your findings to others so you can use the data as part of your decision-making process. Like test scores and attendance rates, the hard data we are more familiar with, the data that emerges from examination of artifacts is useful only if it is channeled toward school improvement.

Let's take a closer look at each of these three categories of artifacts. In this chapter, we will first identify particular artifacts that can be collected for analysis. Next, we provide procedures and questions to use in both collecting as well as to analyze three examples of district and school artifacts: (1) The District/School Calendar can reveal how districts and schools manage the most precious resource they have, time, looking at the available days for learning; (2) Student Schedules can allow you to examine the school day from the students' perspective; (3) The School Master Schedule can allow you to follow how staff time, talent, and energy are used within your school.

This will be enough to get you started. Once you get the hang of it using these examples, you will be able to find other ways to locate and examine the many untapped sources of data that abound in your school.

ANALYZING THE DISTRICT/SCHOOL CALENDAR

Calendars reveal the first round of information about how districts and schools are managing time and to what extent a district can deliver on its promise to educate all students. To get started, you must first collect and organize information. Get copies of your school calendar. Make sure you find out the total number of days in the teachers' calendars, the total number of days teachers actually teach students, and the total number of days of vacation time or other such days. If your school calendar is simply a list of dates, get a regular monthly calendar so you can physically see the teaching and non-teaching time available in each school year. Should your school have multiple calendars, you can analyze each separately and then merge the information for an overall picture of your school.

The process for analyzing calendars is very simple. Simply mark each teaching day, vacation day, professional development day, early release day, and other categories on the monthly calendar. Then total the amount of time remaining: (1) Look first at certified personnel time to see how much time is available for adult work; (2) Look next at student time to see how much direct time is available for teaching and learning.

It is best to start simple, looking only at the regular calendar year. Once you have that analysis in hand, you can look further at the role of extended time, such as summer school and before/after school learning opportunities to be able to incorporate the impact of those additional hours. In the end, you should have a month-by-month picture of the time available for teaching, including the total number of minutes, hours, and days available for teaching and learning in your school.

Once you have this information in hand, you can then ask questions and use the data you have created to find answers. Be sure to stay within the limits of the data, avoiding the temptation of finding answers beyond the limits of the information you have in your hand. There is plenty to learn without stretching your conclusions.

Among the questions you might ask are:

- How much time—in days, hours—do students actually spend in class studying?
- How much time—in days, hours—do students actually spend weekend, holidays, in-service days?
- How much time—in days, hours—do students actually spend in passing times, pep rallies, game times, assemblies, other?
- How much time—in days, hours—do students actually spend on snow days, fire drills, and any other out-of-class time?
- How much time—in days, hours—do students actually lose each day from class periods for functional tasks such as taking role and collecting homework?
- In the end, how much time is available for teaching and learning?
- What is the quality of the available time in terms of how it is spaced across the weeks and the year?

Once you have collected and analyzed data on the school calendar, you will want to arrange your information in usable form so that it can be shared with a variety of publics. Even if you have little or no control of your calendar at the school site level, having the information available is essential to the process of making the best decisions possible to prove positive context for learning and teaching. You can also share the information with those who do have control of calendar decisions, such as district personnel as well as policy level decision-makers so they can be aware of the total time available for schools, as well as the quality of that time.

ANALYZING STUDENT SCHEDULES

Analyzing sample student schedules can give you a fresh look at school and how students actually view the requirements of the system, both for course taking as well as for use of time. A good way to start this process is to shadow a number of students in your school, selecting students representative of the full range of experiences and programs offered. By living the students' schedules with them, you will start to look differently at your master schedule and the work of the school. In the master schedule analyzed in the case study of Rockdale High School, for example, the adults live from left to right, working for the most part in context of the order of a single discipline, with logical subject-centered progression from grade to grade, skill to skill, within that discipline. Students, on the other hand, cut across the master schedule in an irregular pattern from top to bottom, moving from one subject to the next with each period change. While this might be so obvious that discussion seems foolish, the reality of living this difference in perspectives is quite stark.

A single student schedule is a surprisingly rich source of information. When the authors visited a southern high school to help unravel the all-too-familiar mystery of low achievement, a single student schedule offered insight into some of the issues. By looking at a representative schedule, it was quite clear that students had less than 18 school days per subject assessed. With limited time available for teaching, simply sending instructors for professional development and adopting proven programs, necessary though these strategies were, would not be enough to get students to perform at high levels. Students and teachers alike needed more time in the assessed areas, particularly for students who were significantly behind in their studies. A very simple schedule analysis showed the total number of school days per subject, the total number of 8-hour days per subject, and the percentage of available time used per subject. With this information in hand, policymakers had new information to incorporate into their reform-minded thinking.

In this analysis, we will look in particular at use of time within context of the student day. This analysis can also be understood in the larger sense through analysis of student transcripts and course-taking patterns, the schedule taken to the multiple-year perspective. This is another type of study outside the scope of this work, but it is certainly easy enough to do on your own; one you may choose to undergo in your school.

First, collect and organize information. In order to analyze student schedules systematically, you will have to collect samples of student schedules that are representative of different grades and tracks. Be sure to remove student names and any identifying information, replacing it with the category of program. In addition to the student schedules themselves, you will need to know the time information that will tell you how much time students spend in each subject on their schedule. This will include the calendar analysis (see above) as well as the daily schedule for all different types of days.

Next, analyze the data you have collected by asking tough questions and looking critically at what you find. There are many questions you might ask about how time is used for student achievement, and how time and course requirements are operationalized via the student schedule. Here are questions you might ask to guide your thinking.

How much actual time is available for learning?

- How many total school days are available for learning in a calendar year?
- What are the total daily hour/minutes available for students?
- What is the total number of units of time in a day (how many periods plus homeroom)?
- How much of this daily time is class time? How much is non-class time?
- How much of a student's day is spent in academic time?

- How much of the student day aligns with college prep? With state accountability?
- To what degree is the student using time to access rigorous course-work? What is the student's track placement? Is the student taking college-preparatory classes? Is the student taking higher level math?

What percentage of time is available for learning?

- What percentage of the day is spent in each course?
- What percentage of the day is spent in courses/engaged learning activities versus passing time, lunch, homeroom?
- What percentage of the day is spent in academic courses versus non-academic courses?
- What percentage of the day is spent in courses that include subjects tested by the state: English, writing, mathematics, other?
- What is your best estimate of lost time inside each class session from settling in (take role, other) and preparing to leave (assignment for tomorrow, clock-watching)?

What is the quality of the available time for learning?

- To what degree is the student's school day fragmented?
- How many total moves from place to place does the student make?
- What is the length of class time? Is it enough for hands-on learning?
- What is the student's view of day in relation to flow and cohesiveness of the student's experience (for example, American Literature paired with American History)?

Once you have collected this information, you can use it to think differently both as a school and as a district. When high school teachers in a high-poverty California secondary school saw these results, they changed their perspective on responsibility for teaching literacy. Once teachers could see the time limits if literacy instruction remained solely in English classes, they could understand in a visceral way the impossibility of the task of teaching students who are significantly behind to read at grade level in the time allocated for one course. Armed with this understanding, social studies teachers stepped up to the plate and accepted primary responsibility for teaching persuasive writing, a natural part of their discipline, and were continuing conversations to see what other standards they could "adopt." When science teachers saw the same figures for math instructional time, with their students woefully behind, they too understood the role they needed to play in teaching math as an essential part of their discipline.

ANALYZING THE MASTER SCHEDULE

The master schedule is a mother lode artifact, a rich source of data for conducting a number of different analyses that can help you better understand the use of teacher time, talent, and energy for learning and teaching. It provides answers to two key questions that lie at the heart of teaching and learning: (1) Is good teaching supported within the context provided, or is it constrained? (2) Are all our students receiving a rigorous and challenging education, or are some students receiving a better education than others?

While the calendar analysis and the student schedule analysis are relatively simple, the master schedule analysis offers a wider array of data that can be analyzed from multiple perspectives. For this section of the artifacts analysis chapter, therefore, we will divide the discussion into the following subsections, treating each as a separate process: (1) analyzing the staffing pattern, (2) analyzing the use of available time, (3) analyzing teacher workload, (4) analyzing the rigor level of course offerings, and (5) analyzing teacher quality and equity. Let's look, step by step, at ways to analyze the master schedule to learn more about forces flowing through your school. Analyze the data by asking tough questions and looking critically at what you find.

Analyzing the Staffing Pattern

Every school has a specific number of staffing lines called Full Time Equivalents (FTEs). This term normally refers to certified positions, and for purposes of this discussion we will adopt that definition. In order to begin analyzing the master schedule, you must first know the total number of certified positions that are allocated to the school—the total number of FTEs available for assignment.

You must then decide how many positions you will include in your analysis—administrative and non-administrative, regular allocation and additional allocations such as special education, and so forth. The simplest view is to look only at certified positions, not including administrators. As you get more experience, you can add other positions such as administrative lines as well as non-certified positions involved as teaching assistants, looking in particular at all human resources that could be converted to FTEs for teaching or other certified personnel.

Once you know how many total positions are available to the school, you then need to know what each position is assigned to do—teachers of specific subjects, school counselors, master teachers, including whatever the array of position assignments are as well as the number of people assigned to each position.

When you have collected this information, you are ready to begin asking questions that can be answered by the available data. The following are examples of the kinds of questions you should ask yourself, as well as some of the things to look for as you examine the answers you find. The list is certainly not exhaustive, and you should plan to extend your lists of questions and ideas of what to look for. Here are some questions to start you off on your information-gathering journey.

How many total FTEs are available, and how are they assigned?

- How many total FTEs are assigned to the school?
- What are the categories of positions—disciplines, guidance, special education, other? Teaching versus non-teaching?
- How many FTEs are assigned to each category?
- How many FTEs are aligned with state assessment areas? With postsecondary entrance? With postsecondary success goals?

Are staff assigned equitably to school sites?

- Are numbers of staff assigned to sites by equal formula, or are some allocated extra staff?
- If staffing is unequal, who is advantaged?

Are staff assigned equitably within the school sites?

- What is the ratio of core academic faculty to non-core faculty?
- How many teachers on the staff teach core academic subjects? How many teach non-core, non-academic subjects? What is the ratio of total core academic faculty to total non-core, non-academic faculty (subject matter analysis)?
- How does this ratio compare with expectations for student achievement defined by state and district assessment systems, with SAT/ACT assessments, with college admissions criteria, with state and district standards?
- Are staff assigned equitably across grades and within programs?

What are the total dollars available to the school in the form of FTEs (use real or district average)?

- What is the cost of different categories of FTE use—the cost of FTEs assigned to each category?
- What is the cost of teaching versus non-teaching use of FTEs?
- What is the cost of FTEs aligned with state assessments? With postsecondary entrance? With postsecondary success goals?
- How many minutes of annual FTE use equal the instructional budget? Equal other school budgets?

When you have answers to questions such as these, the next step is to decide how to use the information to improve your school. Obviously, if you're focusing on achieving results in academic achievement, your resources allocated should be tightly aligned with assignments that will produce results in critical academic areas. If there is great misalignment between your school goals and how personnel are assigned, the conditions for teaching are less than optimal, and staff will struggle accordingly to produce students with skills of excellence. Unless students have opportunity to learn and teachers have opportunity to teach, they will be hampered.

The conversations that can occur using this data are intellectual and stimulating because there are no absolute answers to what is best. Thus, struggling with this information can serve as opportunity to build intellectual community among staff, as you struggle collectively to resolve difficult issues. Look carefully for the updraft/downdraft tensions that may be present as you review staffing assignments. Is the staffing allocation aligned with the old sorting mechanisms and Carnegie units of awarding credit for earning a diploma, or is the new system of achievement for all a driving force in staffing allocation? Expect to see both, and take on the challenge of working to harness the tensions between the two systems to make school work for all.

Analyzing the Use of Available Time

Once you know how many FTEs are available to the school, you are ready to look at how much time is available to each staff member individually as well as to the school as a collective. To gather information to answer this question, mark the length of the school day for teachers, including the length of each time period or block so you know exactly how many teaching minutes are available per period. Also, record any time used outside the teaching periods, including passing time, length of lunch period, other time used such as homeroom, and time before and after school. Next, find out how much time teachers have allocated by contract for teaching as well as non-teaching time, such as lunch and prep periods. In the end, you need to be able to identify how much total time is available per day, as well as how much contractual time is available for teaching for teaching or other staff duties. Be sure to know any other contractual limits on use of time, such as annual caps on total classroom teaching time per year.

When the raw information is gathered, start to ask critical questions and answer those questions with the data sitting only a few keystrokes away.

How much total time is available for each individual person to conduct his or her assigned duties?

- School calendar for teachers
- Teacher daily hours employed
- Teacher contract time for teaching

What are staff assigned to do according to the master schedule?

- How much actual daily time is spent on teaching? On planning and professional development? On lunch? On supervision and other duties?

- How much actual annual time is spent on teaching? On planning and professional development? On lunch? On supervision and other duties?
- How much professional development time is available in the calendar year? During the school days and weeks?
- What other categories of work are staff assigned to do?
- What is the ratio of "up" time (teaching time) versus "down" time (non-teaching time) per teacher?
- What is the number of professional staff in teaching assignments that pulls students out of classes (for example, GAT teacher with no students assigned on regular basis) versus teachers with regular assignments?

How does the staff time look when presented as percentages of available time?

- What percentage of actual daily time is spent on teaching? On planning and professional development? On lunch? On supervision and other duties?
- What percentage of actual annual time is spent on teaching? On planning and professional development? On lunch? On supervision and other duties?
- What percentage of time is available for professional development in the calendar year? During the school days and weeks? During the regular school day?
- What are the categories of work staff are assigned to do by percentage of total available staff time, talent, and energy?

How does the staff time look when presented as cost of time spent on different duties?[1]

- What is the daily cost of staff time spent on teaching? On planning and professional development? On lunch? On supervision and other duties?

---

1. Cost can be calculated using actual staff salary/benefits, or it can be calculated using average district salary/benefits.

- How much annual cost of time spent on teaching? On planning and professional development? On lunch? On supervision and other duties?
- What is the cost of professional development time available in the calendar year? During the school days and weeks?
- What is the cost of different categories of work that staff are assigned to do by categories, such as the cost of work that directly aligns with state assessments? With teaching versus non-teaching?

Once you start to think this way, you can ask questions about various categories of work, depending on what makes sense for your situation, and can answer your questions using the staff assignments found on a school master schedule. To the extent that assigned duties are not listed on the master schedule, such as lunchroom duty, you can supplement the data with that information. The idea is to get the most accurate, most detailed picture of what teachers and other staff members are assigned to do each day, each week, or each cycle, and then to combine that information in many different ways. By looking at categories of work staff are assigned to do, you can gain insight into your core values as an institution, into what is valued most highly in relation to the public purpose of schooling, and what is valued most highly in relation to the historic role of schools in sorting students into categories of success and failure.

Analyzing Teacher Workload

Teacher workload is a huge factor in supporting or constraining effective teaching. While improving the context in which teacher work cannot guarantee or create quality teaching, expecting teachers to teach in a situation with impossible workloads is certain to erode the quality of instruction over time.

In order to look at teacher workload, first make sure you find out the class sizes for every class taught in the school. When teachers have times without students other than contractual time, mark that class size zero. Once you have class sizes for every teacher, total the student contacts each teacher has per day, and put that figure on the master schedule. The idea here is to look at capacity for personalization, linking the total number of students a teacher must know well as learners with the context in which they work due to the numbers of students they must know.

When you have gathered this information, ask yourselves critical questions to help you understand the impact of teacher-student load on teachers and teaching.

Does the total daily and weekly teaching load make excellent teaching possible?

- What are your teachers' total number of student contacts per day? Are you allowing for teachers to have a load that makes teaching possible?
- Is the distribution of total teacher contact load even across all programs, or is total teacher contact load unevenly distributed? If the load is unevenly distributed, are there patterns in characteristics of programs, students, and track? Who has the lowest number of total contacts? Who has the greatest?
- Does the teaching load make assigning and scoring quality homework possible? For example, if a teacher gives an assignment to every student he or she teaches in a day and every student completes that assignment, how much total time (in hours and minutes) will it take for the teacher to grade it? Is this time expectation reasonable? Does this time vary from one program to another? From one track to another?
- How many different preps do teachers have? What is the level of difficulty of those preps? Do teachers have a program that is already developed, or are they developing a new program?

Does the classroom teaching load make excellence in teaching possible?

- What is the class size? Is it the same for all, or does it vary from program to program? From track to track? From grade to grade?
- What is the class composition in relation to span of different achievement levels, and percentages of students in each level of performance? In relation to regular and special education ratios? English language learners (ELL) student ratios?
- What is the annual percentage of classroom stability? How many students are enrolled in the class throughout the year? In the school throughout the year? What is the multi-year student stability rate?

- What is the nature of classroom enrollment turnover? Do the same students come in and out, or do new students come in and out?
- Do teachers teach in multiple years (for example, looping versus new class each year)?

Do teachers have flexibility in making decisions about class size and total student contacts?

- Can teachers adjust class size?
- Can teachers adjust total number of students they see per year?
- Is flexibility in adjusting class size ongoing, or is it "one-time-only?"
- Do teachers have flexibility in grouping and regrouping students for a variety of purposes?

Do teachers receive supports for working with students who have special needs?

- What supports are available for teachers?
- How are special education, ELL, and other support teachers used (inclusion versus direct instruction)?

How much time is required to prepare for teaching outside the school day?

- What is the total scoring time required for an assignment for all students? About 5 minutes per paper? About10 minutes per paper?
- How many separate preparations do teachers have?
- How many new preparations do teachers have?

Once you have collected and analyzed information according to these and other questions, you will have solid data that informs you and your school about the situation in which teachers are working. Lack of time is a voice heard loud, clear, and often in relation to the teaching profession, and once you look directly at the data for your whole school you will have a chance to make decisions that will let you use collective time with greater care.

While analyzing the use of staff time in several middle schools in one district, one of the authors found a total of more than four full FTEs significantly underutilized across most sites. By gathering fragments of time wasted across the day and the year, the schools were able to create a three-hour professional development block for every staff member in the school every week, in addition to the regular planning time already in place. Furthermore, middle school students were able to engage in individualized work in courses such as art, music, and tech ed while their teachers were in professional development improving their instructional skills, so both teacher and student learning opportunities were enriched—a "win-win" change resulting from looking at the use of staff time as data.

Analyzing the Rigor Level of Course Offerings (see also chapter 6)

In addition to looking at how teacher time is used in the master schedule, you can also look at the collective student time spent in rigorous coursework for the school as a whole. A very simple way to kick off this type of thinking is to analyze the course offerings, looking to see what proportion of courses are high track, general track, and low track. In some instances, this will be easy—courses will be marked with terms such as "AP English" or "Basic English." In other instances, schools may say that they don't track, and that all courses are the same. This may be true, and all courses may be taught in true heterogeneous fashion to a truly mixed group of students. In other cases, however, there may actually be differences in the courses despite the formal description. You may have to locate other artifacts that support the master schedule, such as course descriptions found in student course selection documents, in order to categorize courses accurately.

The secret here is to be blatantly honest. Some courses may be described the same way, for example, yet pre-college students may be served primarily in one group while special needs students are served primarily in another. In this instance, the courses would be tracked, despite course description.

Once you have this information, you can ask key questions such as: What types of classes are offered?

*What categories of courses are offered, and
what is the percentage of each category?*

- How many total classes taught in the school are core academic classes?
- How many are non-core?
- What is the ratio of total core academic classes taught to total non-core, non-academic classes taught?

When you analyze this data, look carefully for the tensions between offering rigorous classes as well as for classes that provide students who are behind with densely packed opportunity to close the achievement gap. And, on the other hand, look for patterns in course offerings that actually increase inequity in achievement, exacerbating any existing gap in achievement for all. Look for courses that have historically been included as part of the Carnegie unit system of graduation requirements, remnants of the sorting system, yet that fail to align with skills needed for success in postsecondary schools. You have opportunity, once you identify these patterns, to change the courses offered, or to change the content and rigor level of courses that may still be required by the state for graduation, but offer low level contribution to student achievement.

Analyzing Teacher Quality and Equity

In analyzing teacher quality and equity in student access to the highest performing teachers, the key question was asked several years ago by Joe Murphy—"Who is being taught by whom?" In looking for updraft/downdraft dynamics, the key issue is distribution of teachers. Do all students have quality teachers, or are the highest qualified teachers assigned to students who have historically succeeded in school, while students at greatest risk are assigned the least qualified teachers?

If available, it's good to know the years' experience of each teacher, the degree level achieved, and the certification area(s) of each teacher in order to examine differences in teacher assignment and to look for trends such as in-field and out-of-field teaching. It may or may not be possible to get this type of data, or to get all of it. Once you have gathered the available data, you can ask questions.

What is "teacher quality" and how do we recognize it?

- What is degree level of certified personnel?
- What is the quality of the teacher preparation program? Is program accredited?
- What is the quality of content knowledge preparation? What are majors/minors?

What number and level of courses did teacher take for subject teaching?

- Are teachers in field versus out of field?

Are teachers experienced or inexperienced?

- How many total years' experience does each certified staff member have?
- How many total years experience in the school does each certified staff member have?
- How many total years in the field does each certified staff member have?

Are teachers assigned to programs of equal quality, or are there inequalities in qualifications of staff assigned?

- Are more qualified teachers assigned to students most in need or to students most advantaged?
- Are staff members assigned to schools of equal quality, or are there inequalities in qualifications of staff assigned?
- Are more qualified teachers assigned to schools most in need or to schools most advantaged?

Is the staff stable, or is there high mobility?

- What is the school annual turnover rate in relation to the district? To surrounding districts? To the state? The nation?

- What are the number of regular staff versus long-term subs versus series of short-term subs?
- What is the teacher absentee rate? Does it vary according to differences in program assignment? In track assignment?
- Are substitutes provided equitably across all programs when teachers are absent, or do other teachers have to absorb students?
- What is quality of substitute force?

Once you have gathered and analyzed this data, be ready for some difficult conversations. As the research clearly shows, parents of the more advantaged students go after the strongest teachers for their students, a key factor in creating updraft for their children. This leaves the least qualified teachers for students who are more likely to be in the downdraft, focusing their attention at best on graduating from high school. In addition, veteran teachers with higher level credentials tend to flock to the higher track courses such as the Advanced Scholars Program, while new teachers take the assignments that are left.

Confronting these issues opens the door to discussing issues that are most often ignored in secondary schools, the thorny and politically loaded conversations about teacher quality and the hierarchy of power among teachers. It opens the door to conversations about some teachers being more qualified, and others less qualified. In terms of teacher experience and degree levels, the conversation is rather straightforward, supported by differences in pay structure that are a normal part of school culture. When you get into the more contentious arenas such as level of content knowledge and ability to produce results in student achievement, discussions about teacher quality and assignment of teachers can become quite emotional.

Remember, you are looking for updraft/downdraft dynamics with this data and using the information to improve schools for all. Even though it is a very tough conversation to have, harnessing the power of struggle with real challenges can create intellectual community that moves all staff to higher levels of success.

NEXT STEPS IN ANALYZING ARTIFACTS

In conclusion, artifacts are abundant sources of information about what is happening in your schools. You can begin by simply analyzing each type of artifact mentioned earlier to see if there is equal opportunity for teachers to hold high expectations and equal opportunity for students to achieve those expectations.

AT LEAST TWO WAYS TO UNEARTH DATA

1) Identifying and analyzing more artifacts as sources of data

You will find many new possibilities in terms of thinking about available data—course selection documents, course syllabi, letters to parents from different diploma tracks, assessments used in different tracks as well as the frequency and intensity of the assessments scheduled, use of time within the period, and on and on. As you identify and explore sources of data, it will be helpful for you to consider the data analysis process used here—focus on organizing data and then asking critical questions to create usable data. Keep track of your questions, so they can serve others as well as help you with consistency from year to year.

2) Making connections across the data from different artifacts

You will begin to make connections across the different categories of artifacts. For one, assess the impact of combining the number of days available from the calendar with the total number of hours available for instruction in a single subject. If you combine the daily time available to learn a single subject within the calendar days available and convert that to the number of school days available if you spent the whole day doing that one subject, you will get an entirely different feel for time available for learning. You might compare core to non-core time in context of the calendar, and then go on to analyze the impact of interruptions in the calendar. What is the impact of teachers teaching 5 periods while others teach 6 periods in adding to differences in ratios of teachers assigned to programs? The possibilities are endless!

Once you have the data in your hand in a solid way, you may find that the results are overwhelming. How can we hold high expectations for all, when powerful updraft/downdraft forces push differentiated opportunity to learn and differentiated expectations?

While creating context that constrains learning and teaching is a huge mistake, simply creating positive context is not enough. There are all too many examples of secondary structural change that become the main goal, change that occurs without focusing on the underlying purpose for the change—situating learners and teachers in a context that improves their ability to learn and teach. Let's move on the last section in search of answers to this dilemma, looking at using artifact analysis to focus on the classroom.

6

How to Analyze Curriculum and Instruction

A high school diploma should again become a mark of accomplishment, not simply recognition of seat time accumulated.

—National Commission on the High School Senior Year 2001

The opportunity to learn challenging material and to acquire the personal and academic skills that it takes to master a subject well depends in great part on what happens inside the classroom on a daily basis. Consequently, learning plays out as a partnership between curriculum and instruction. Teachers determine the quality and effectiveness of the partnership during the planning and delivery stages of the curriculum. What teachers teach in curricular terms and how those lessons are translated through instruction are archived inside artifacts that can be studied for clues about how the curriculum and instruction assist or impede learning.

GRADE 9

Guided reading of classics including *Romeo and Juliet,* the *Odyssey* and *Call of the Wild.* Comprehension and interpretation. Daily spelling, vocabulary. Descriptive writing, planning and outlining; capitalization, and punctuation. Pre-algebra tools for algebra and geometry with emphasis on equations, factors, rationals, functions, graphing and ratio. Earth science, with focus on minerals, rocks, landforms, erosion, earthquakes, volcanoes, atmosphere, climate, oceanography and astronomy. Health and personal hygiene. History of the United States from its beginning to 1877. History of sculpture (Trent Academy 2001).

Curriculum is the "stuff" of learning. It's the content framed inside a discipline. It's the collective effect of the topics, reading materials, assignments, and supporting experiences arranged in a scope and sequence that largely determine the rigor of the course. Instruction translates that stuff into learning. In the current educational arena, state and local standards provide a set of parameters that frame curricula with broad statements about what all students should know and be able to do. In addition, state and exit assessments measure learning aligned to state and local standards. In high school another set of parameters influences curricula: Carnegie units. In this system, courses are measured by time (3 hours = 3 units) as well as coverage of topics in the discipline. The dual dynamics of coverage and standards may pressure high schools to go for either coverage or for rigor, while in some cases courses are successful in meeting both sets of demands. AP courses fall into this category. More often than not, though, staff is cornered by the rigor versus units tension inside the secondary curriculum.

Another way state and local policies influence curricula involves the number of courses required for graduation. In one state, students are required to accumulate credits in nineteen areas during the high school years. Such regulations create curriculum sprawl and force teachers into a survival mode particularly when they are seeing large numbers of students each day. Those students who arrive at the secondary school with weak literacy and numerical skills are especially vulnerable to the effects of this sprawl. They must hop from course to course, several of which do not have much to do with postsecondary expectations. Consequently, they do not have the option to spend time in the core areas when they must meet so many requirements. As a result, schools may develop ways to "cheat teach," a term we overheard used by high school and college students who were describing defensive teaching. They referred to the superficial treatment of subject matter and other short-hand methods that prod and prop students through the curriculum without "really teaching." When analyzing a curriculum for effectiveness and rigor, then, the analysis must look at what is actually being taught.

This analysis involves artifacts used to document curricula and to teach, including student work, syllabi, and lesson plans. These artifacts can reveal the level of challenge, engagement, practice, and relevance that students need to pursue next steps on the curricular ladder and to prepare for assessments. One vitally important feature relating to equity and excellence involves the opportunity to learn through effort. Effort demands that students use multiple mental and intellectual skills to learn, as well as have the time to practice and apply these concepts and skills (Resnick 2000). Curricula based in the approach that learning is a product of time and effort levels the playing field, so to speak, and makes learning possible and from the student's point of view, trustworthy. Another important feature of the curriculum to look for is explicitness. Courses and teaching that clearly describe the expectations of the course using rubrics and other means of communicating the tasks and the expectations also support students in their effort to succeed at rigorous coursework.

An analysis of curriculum and instruction demands a somewhat different mental task and set of questions than the analyses with schedules. This analysis pursues questions around what is valued and how that is expressed in documentation, such as curriculum guides and course descriptions. We are not dealing with numbers and quantifiable features so the language we use may appear less exact and perhaps less certain. For one, curriculum and instruction take us into questions about what is good teaching and how do we know it when we see it? For our purposes, we describe good teaching as effective teaching.

When we look at curricular and instructional documentation we look for evidence in, say, how the curriculum advances learning from level to level in the discipline and how it prepares students for a variety of assessments: final exams, major papers, mid-terms, state assessments, college admissions exams. Since successful completion—in terms of performance and units—of a course or set of courses is the goal for every student, the curriculum analysis should consider both the content structure and management structures involving time and effort to support student performance. As an artifact, for example, a curriculum guide or master course catalog sends messages about expectations and demands—the "toughness" or lack thereof of the high school experience. A reading of course descriptions can flag questions around rigor. Take the following two descriptions from the same course catalog from a large urban district's curriculum guide for high schools.

Low-Rigor versus High-Rigor Course Descriptions

Office Reprographics	AP U.S. Government
Teaches various methods of duplication. Students make copies of any finished product, describing the best form of duplication for the number of copies needed. Trains students to use machines commonly found in business offices. Since the need for duplicating and copying equipment has increased over the years, every secretary should be familiar with different kinds of machines and processes available for making copies.	Offers opportunity for college credit from participating universities to students who perform well on the Advanced Placement examination. The course provides a college level survey of American government and politics as well as comparative government and politics. A variety of approaches, materials, and concepts are available to the teacher from the College Board.

These two descriptions of courses offered at the same high school are quick indicators of the wide variance in content, instruction, and opportunity inside the larger curriculum. To take this further, what is the ratio of core to non-core offerings? What does this say about the high school experience and access to postsecondary preparation?

Curriculum alone is a static thing. Instruction enlivens curriculum and makes it powerful, or not. Although the effectiveness of instruction is often measured by student achievement data, instruction can be blamed unnecessarily if we do not consider the contexts surrounding instructional opportunity. Is there enough time to teach "deeply"? Do teachers have appropriate materials? Have they had the training to deliver new methods or systems of instruction? An analysis of the curricular context must look at how each element acts responsibly in delivering the learning experience.

INSTRUCTIONAL DENSITY

Effective instruction has "density." That is, it has a quality of focus and intensity that engulfs the learner in new knowledge and yet allows for practice and exploration. Instructional density enables the learner to move through an iterative process, one that allows for learning and relearning. We call this condition "instructional density" because we want to capture that sense of immersion or, to use a current vogue description, of "going deep" into content. Instructional density supports, augments, enlivens, and focuses curriculum—it makes it come alive and makes it engaging. Effective teachers employ instructional density through a set of teaching practices and routines that create a deeper understanding of key concepts and skills. National research underscores the value of students enrolling in the more rigorous and engaging courses that employ instructional density.

A growing body of research demonstrates that students learn more, and learning is distributed more equitably, in schools with a constrained curriculum, consisting largely of academic courses and with few low-level courses. In such "constrained curriculum" schools, students typically are required to complete many of these courses to graduate. (Lee and Burkam 2000)

When we include curriculum and instruction in our bag of artifacts, the analysis becomes trickier, but we will discuss several ways to use curricular artifacts.

CURRICULUM

The Curriculum Guide

Every high school has a curriculum guide. This document contains the course descriptions offered at a school and, in effect, provides documentation that reveals what choices students have, how the curriculum as a whole emphasizes rigorous coursework, how the high school tracks or categorizes students, and to what degree support classes are offered. Some guides include letters or introductory material from the principal or school board; these materials can identify assumptions, attitudes, beliefs and goals. In some cases, the curriculum guide does not provide enough information, and so other documents may have to be pursued.

The importance of monitoring curriculum is underscored by research showing the longer a student stays in a high-poverty school, the less likely student will enroll in rigorous, college-preparatory courses and study challenging coursework (Adelman 2001). Key questions raised by a curriculum guide include:

- What is the ratio between core courses and extra-curricular courses?
- Are there multiple levels of courses within a subject, such as Algebra 1?
- Are core courses divided into qualitatively differing sets of classes with more and less rigorous demands? For example, can freshmen science credits be satisfied with either Biology or Environmental Science?

The Syllabus

The syllabus provides information about the scope and sequence of a course and can provide information about alignments to standards, coverage, and specific topics. By comparing syllabi in the same strand (i.e. Algebra I), a school can ask questions about course-to-course alignment. The syllabus provides feedback on vertical and horizontal alignments with standards and assessments.

- Do intra-course syllabi align with the same standards?
- Do intra-course syllabi use the same performance criteria or if not, do criteria add up to appropriate and equal demands?
- Does coursework include an appropriate set of reading materials? An analysis of a syllabus in ninth grade English might show that the course uses books already taught in middle school.
- Do other ninth grade English courses teach different sets of books of a higher or lower demand? If so, why?

A Comparison of Public and Private High Schools' English Courses

High School A (from a West Coast public school district curriculum guide:

PERSONALIZATION:

As part of the personalization of high school, an examination of the high school experience has been woven into the six units of study that have been designed for ninth grade English classes. All students will participate in these personalization activities that will set the tone for the rest of their time in high school. The units of study and the high school experience components are listed below.

- *Unit 1 — Building Community: Fiction Text.* Who are we as a high school class? What does high school mean to me? (Writing component).
- *Unit 2 — Research (I-Search): Biographies (Non-fiction).* Who am I as a high school student and how does high school fit with who I am now and who I want to become? The School-to-Career and Counseling offices will serve as research sources.
- *Unit 3 — Response to Literature: Fiction.* How do writers reflect/not reflect who I am and what I want to be? How do authors attempt to shape who I am or want to be? What role does literacy play in who I want to become? What do I need to know and be able to do as a reader and writer? What are my plans for ensuring I have the skills I need if I want to go to college?
- *Unit 4 — Feature Articles: Non-fiction Text.* Who do I want to become? Students will research a topic or issue of interest that is related to their future plans and aspirations.
- *Unit 5 — Informational Text: Non-fiction.* What else do I need to know to become the person I want to be? Students will conduct a second I-Search for careers.
- *Unit 6 — "My Turn" Essays: Persuasive Text.* What do I believe? How do I fit into the larger context beyond the classroom and school site?

High School B - Ninth grade syllabus
(from a West Coast private high school):

English I is an introduction to literature and composition. The course introduces the four basic genres of literature: poetry, drama, fiction (both short stories and novels), and non-fiction. It also lays a foundation for understanding the development of the Western tradition in literature, beginning with the Greeks notably Sophocleantragedy and continuing through the Renaissance, particularly Shakespeare, and the Victorian period to the contemporary.

Major course assessments:

- There will be essays during every unit.
- Students will write journal responses that require them to critically analyze aspects of the literature that they read.
- Occasionally there will be quizzes in order to check that students are keeping up with the reading.
- Class participation will be a factor.
- There will be a final exam that covers all of the literature from the first semester.

- What standards (Response to Literature; Writing a Research Paper, other) are addressed?
- Do courses cover a range of standards or just a few?
- How are they measured—written tasks, oral tasks, multiple-choice tests, quizzes, posters, other?
- Is there a common end-of-course exam?

The Assignment

Assignments, or tasks, are invaluable sources of information about rigor and appropriateness. An analysis of a single task can provide a focus for professional development as well as a break down of the instructional strategies and methods employed by teachers. This process leads staff to question and monitor the effectiveness of instructional choices. Consistent analysis can provide rich data around how instruction and curriculum support learning or impede it; how instruction varies or not; whether rigor is consistently embedded in tasks; and whether departments are delivering the same expectations inside of those tasks to all students. If not, is there a rationale?

One method for using assignments as data was designed by Hollingsworth and Ybarra at Data Works Educational Research. A school collects tasks over a period of time then calibrates these tasks to grade level, and so this method is called "calibration." For example, a middle school collected all tasks that involved writing over a three week period. An outside group indicated the grade level appropriateness of each assignment and then tallied the results. The vast majority of these tasks calibrated at the elementary level, with the most common tasks involving fill-in-the blank worksheets. It was clear that no one at any grade level was receiving sufficient opportunity to write in response to literature, to write in science or social studies class, or to do multiple drafts. In fact, assignments involving writing an essay were virtually non-existent at this school at any grade. The calibration exercise provided a fairly stunning set of indicators about the state of writing at the school. The correlation between low state assessment scores and curriculum and instruction became quite obvious.

There are other ways to inventory tasks to track how aligned the daily work of the curriculum is with the "bigger" picture using both standards and assessments. Using a collection of tasks, correlate assignments to standards to determine which standards are being addressed. If this collection involves a term or even a semester, staff can see whether tasks address a narrow range of standards (for example, conventions in English) or a wider range (for example, synthesis of themes in two poems).

Another way to use a collection is to correlate assignments against state assessments, SATs, and exit exams. Each assessment provides information on the type and frequency of items, providing staff with information about how to prepare students for the content and format of these tests. For one, the SAT is very much a vocabulary test. Students who have large vocabularies have an advantage, clearly, over students with low vocabularies. A calibration that sets up key activities aligned with specific exams would uncover how well matched the course and its assignments are with what students must know to do well on these gate keeping assessments (Dougherty 2001).

INSTRUCTION

Instruction is described as both an art and a science. People like to argue whether it's the product of good pedagogy or good content. Of course, the truth is probably somewhere in between. There are attempts to describe, even measure, good teaching using sets of principles or benchmarks, and performance evaluations at least try to describe what a teacher does. Artifacts that play a part in daily teaching, particularly lesson plans, assignments and student work, indicate the level of rigor, the role of effort, the explicitness of the delivery of the course, and to some extent the methodology.

Assignments can help a staff understand how the curriculum looks at the micro-level. Assignments can also help staff look at the effectiveness of teaching methods coupled with assignments. A protocol developed by Ruth Mitchell does just that; it analyzes a task accompanied by the entire set of student work. This collaborative process called Standards In Practice helps make visible what is working or what isn't working for students (Mitchell 1998). It might be that the task is unclear or that the demands are too low or uninteresting or superficial. This process ultimately looks at teacher work and gives the teacher information that will allow him or her to correct instruction (National Staff Development Council describes four such protocols in Tools for Schools, February/March 2001). If this analysis is done frequently, staff can keep track of how effective instructional strategies and tools are for students.

An inventory of instructional practices can also provide information to staff about the level of variety used inside the school. This inventory should include such descriptors as lecture, small group work, field work, problem-based learning and research, note-taking, video productions, and guest speakers. Oral and technology-based work might also be included. The frequency of use would also provide useful information. The goal may not be to employ all methods but an inventory may reveal that students spend a large amount of their time listening to teachers talk and taking notes, for example. Staff can use this information to decide if other strategies are needed or some should be dropped.

Lesson Plans

Lesson plans can also lead to questions about the delivery of a course and the appropriateness of instructional choices. When demanding curricula fails, the culprit can probably be found in the day-to-day teaching choices. Lesson plans should be evolutionary in the sense they allow for those serendipitous moments in the classroom when a teacher decides to "carpe diem." On the other hand, no lesson plans or very broad ones probably mean teachers are unclear about how to deliver the content of the course.

- Is the course dependent on textbook exercises?
- Is instruction of one mode or does the teaching employ multiple modes?
- How often are students engaged in writing assignments?
- Is there reading required in all subjects?
- Are lessons constructed for coverage, or for depth of learning?
- Does instruction embed the demands of standards and assessments?
- Is the course interesting and relevant to students?

Key Exams and Grades

By examining those course assignments (mid-terms, finals, larger projects, portfolios), schools can check to see if mid-terms and final exams or projects are aligned to standards, are rigorous, and contain skills and knowledge students need to know to do well on state assessments and college entrance exams. Key is whether grades and state assessment scores are in alignment. Obviously, if the majority of students receive high grades in English, for example, but the school's assessment scores are in the bottom levels, then there is a mismatch in expectations.

- Do course exams align vertically with next level courses: for example, Algebra I prepares students for advanced level mathematics in Geometry or Algebra II?

- Do exams align with the demands of SAT and ACT admissions exams?
- Do exams and other class work prepare students for placement exams? Military exams? Technical college exams?
- Do grades align with scores on state assessments and other key exams?
- Does the plan follow an appropriate sequence?

Professional Development

Professional development will make or break the effectiveness of curriculum and instruction. An analysis of training schedules and programs offered at the school and in the district can reveal the bonds between professional development, curriculum demands and student achievement. For one, training in areas where students are held accountable provides a strong connection to student achievement.

- What kinds of training are offered?
- Does training relate to areas where student achievement is weak?
- Do all teachers receive training in teaching of reading and writing?
- How much time is allotted to collaborative planning and self-monitoring?
- Is professional development embedded inside daily practices?
- Is there a coaching model?
- What is the ratio of training hours in assessed areas to other training hours?
- What amount of faculty meeting and planning time includes professional development in core subject areas?

Analyzing Documents for Messages about What Matters

An artifact analysis can be a dual search for what you need to know and what you don't know. That is, your search may reveal patterns of course differences within a subject area during a search conducted to inventory what texts are used inside sections of a course. At times, searching through artifacts reveals a set of data that simply puts information on the table, to be questioned and interpreted. Other times, staff can direct an analysis around a specific criterion. For example, an analysis of lessons plans might look at writing tasks; another might involve a survey of instructional methods that considers how teachers use dialog in the classroom. An analysis often provides both information that serves to track patterns and trends, while simultaneously saying something about what the school values. If learning rigorous coursework is expected for all students, then the curricula and their supporting elements will tell a specific story. In this sense, a search through artifacts involves uncovering evidence about what the school values. If a school's main function is merely to get students through the system, one might expect to find a higher number of non-core offerings. We have already seen the two descriptions of courses earlier in this chapter. If we highlight key words inside the text, the messages about what's valued and what's expected become clear.

Likewise, documents circulated to staff, students, and parents are artifacts acting as both sources of hard data—for example, ratio of AP to non-credit courses—or as evidence of beliefs and attitudes that effect learning and teaching. What messages school communities communicate provide strong evidence of what is valued. Is it academic success? Is it harmony and politeness? Is it sport championships?

SOME IMAGES OF EFFECTIVE CURRICULUM AND INSTRUCTION

Our position is that effective curriculum and instruction prepares students to perform at proficient or better levels set by state and national standards in the content areas as well as to be able to move into next level course sequences. Consequently, staff needs to start analyzing this area by looking closely at achievement data.

Once the staff determines where pockets of effectiveness reside inside the data, then some methods for determining what happened in those areas and how teachers managed curriculum and instruction would be worthwhile. Researchers and schools who have done this have arrived at some useful descriptions to speed the thinking along. Effective curriculum and instruction deliver the learning experiences that allow and inspire students to take on the demands of standards and content. Quality curricula and instruction are imperative if we are to create the outcomes for students that an inventory of teaching practices begs attention. What quality teaching is or is not is controversial and is often avoided in secondary schools because it tends to ignite passions more than reason. Nevertheless, it is worthwhile getting to what constitutes effective teaching in a school in order to better understand how to shape the context for effective teaching. It's important to note that studies seem to show that high quality curriculum and materials alone do not improve student achievement if instruction is weakly aligned to those materials and curriculum. We cannot avoid trying to understand these dynamics if we are to move more and more students out of the downdraft and into the updraft of academic achievement.

The research points emphatically at the critical effects of poor versus effective teaching. In one study, elementary students who received ineffective teaching in consequetive years fell further and further behind (Education Trust 2000). By secondary school, these students face daunting challenges if they are to catch up. They must deal with a system that has constructed its learning environments to meet predominately the requirements of secondary policy rather than the needs of students: 47-minute classes, 19 subject areas, large classes, few, if any, instruction or support in reading or writing. Likewise, teachers face the equally daunting task of meeting their needs inside these structures of time, space, resources and regulations.

Research from studies of K–12 teaching provide some images and language to describe what effective curriculum and instruction look like, as opposed to fragmented lessons and defensive teaching. According to research (Lauger 2001; Haberman 1995; Walker 2000; Appleby 2001; Chall 2000), effective curriculum and instruction involve knowledge, behaviors, practices, attitudes and pedagogical skills that:

- Provide explicit instruction
- Use classroom routines
- Challenge and involve students
- Engage in constructive student–teacher classroom climate
- Use a discursive style and create a discursive environment
- Craft many stimulating curricular activities
- Display student work prominently
- Use clearly formulated instructional strategies
- Monitor progress and give feedback

- Have in-depth knowledge of reading and writing processes and how to teach them
- Place high demands and expectations
- Create intellectual excitement; consider alternative points of view
- Emphasize logical and strategy-oriented instruction, clear writing, critical thinking
- Persist in finding ways to engage all students in learning activities
- Protect learners and learning
- Use generalization to provide students with goals or the big picture
- Believe teachers bear the primary responsibility for learning
- Are professional in their approach to students
- Allow for failure and fallibility
- Coach rather than engage in directive teaching
- Emphasize student effort over ability
- Engage in planning
- Expect and accommodate a range of differences
- Employ a demanding teaching style
- Work with the assumption that the teacher's job is to be certain that students learn the material presented
- Identify implicitly with students' needs and aspirations
- Understand how to negotiate the world beyond the local community
- Make learning cumulative and reinforcing
- Gear instruction to helping students enter into the curricular conversation
- Create a larger whole so that students can continue the curricular conversation each day
- Use instructional scaffolding supported by an appropriate breadth of materials
- Use a traditional, teacher-centered, not student-centered, approach producing higher academic achievement

One researcher sums it up this way: "Effective teachers have a sense of what they are doing and why, and they create within their classrooms a sense of coherence and direction that students recognize (and, indeed, to which students also contribute)" (Appleby 2001). An analysis of curricula and instruction promotes an awareness of the dynamics inside teaching and learning, and by knowing what these experiences look like and how they play out, staff and leadership can better monitor their work and make necessary corrections as they progress through each school year. Such an analysis would provide invaluable information for developing school improvement plans, for one. It is also an opportunity to consider, and reconsider, how teaching becomes effective and stays that way, and how future generations of teachers can benefit from these findings. The next chapter provides a more specific image of what actions schools are taking, or could take, to further their efforts to improve academic achievement for all students.

7

Creating Updraft for All—Bold, Bolder, Boldest!

Dare the school build a new social order?

—George S. Counts 1932

While daunting, don't despair if you find updraft/downdraft dynamics in your schools. For schools and communities who have the will to improve, there is help available both from the research as well as from the wisdom of practice. Michael Barber and Vicki Phillips (2000) offer an intriguing viewpoint, suggesting that the secret to success in school reform is to harness the power of the tension in strong opposites, rather than giving up in the face of intractable problems:

> It is our conviction that the conflicts, the setbacks, and the disappointments arise from a single, constantly repeating error. Over and over again important, potentially transforming ideas—equity and diversity, pressure and support, innovation and stability, actions and beliefs—have been placed in opposition to each other. . . . As a result, the potential for transformation is lost. The more effective course of action, which is supported both by the evidence and our own experience, is to allow these apparent opposites to work in concert to create radical change. Bringing together ideas that are often considered to be opposites—what we are calling "fusion" in this paper—can unleash irreversible change for the better. It is that simple—and that difficult! (p. 1)

In this final chapter, we offer food for thought as you struggle to harness the power in the tension between two strong systems to move your school into greater success for all, rather than giving up because the tension is so daunting. We first continue our visit to the research, looking for powerful underlying dynamics that, harnessed wisely, can help offset the updraft/downdraft phenomenon so that all teaching and learning occurs in an updraft. Finally, we visit ideas for creating a more equitable future, looking at bold, bolder, and boldest ideas for tackling stratifying forces by maximizing the press for high achievement for all.

RESEARCH-BASED INSIGHTS INTO CREATING ACADEMIC UPDRAFT FOR ALL

In addition to identifying forces that can negatively impact success, the high school research gives us insights into powerful change levers that can shift the school from an updraft/downdraft setting for learning to a strong and persistent updraft context for all.

Pressing teachers to improve instruction without attending to the realities of these classroom dynamics narrows the range of possibility for significantly improving practice. Used creatively to make improved decisions about teaching and learning, this information offers levers to reverse the tides of negative achievement. The lessons the research teaches us can lead to change.

1. Accept Responsibility

Accepting responsibility for student achievement gives teachers power to take action. Engaged, quality teachers are the linchpins of the successful high school. If students are to learn, teachers must engage in the hard work of quality teaching as the secret to opening the door of engaging students in learning. Teachers engage when they believe their work is important and because they believe that learning is possible. Teachers' sense of possibility is tied directly to their belief that they have the capacity to influence how well students learn—a term called "efficacy." It is this sense of efficacy, teachers' belief in self, that allows teachers to accept responsibility for student achievement, regardless of who their students are. And it is accepting responsibility for student achievement that empowers teachers to take action. Efficacy strongly impacts teacher effort, goal-orientation, level of aspiration, persistence, resilience, openness to new ideas, commitment to teaching, and levels of planning and organization. Accepting responsibility is thus a powerful and essential tool for student achievement.

The key to accepting responsibility is knowing what that responsibility is about and what the challenges are in clear, unambiguous terms. Using data in multiple forms—artifacts, state and district achievement data, and other indicators—communicates to all within the school community what the problem is and where the leverages for change are. Data also track progress and let schools know what is and isn't working.

For teachers to accept responsibility, leadership in the schools and district must create the opportunities for people to come together to analyze and revisit the data. Collectively, the team should look for places inside high schools where practices are working for students and rethinking those that don't. One way to initiate this iterative process is to use the school's strategic plan to provide the basis for reflection and analysis. These plans reveal where alignments between and within the structural and academic parts of the middle and high school systems are occurring or not. This thinking involves a decidedly messy process as it must consider hard facts through the data and sometimes questions previous decisions. Unfortunately, those who wish it to be neat, linear and compartmentalized can derail good strategic thinking and planning in their effort to keep these sessions "harmonious" and the decisions simple. Instead, it is a creative, divergent kind of thinking and planning that constantly renegotiates its decisions based on the effectiveness of those decisions and their outcomes.

Accepting responsibility also means never being satisfied with last year's results. When gains are made inside the school, the school community should set new goals. If one group of students made gains, set new goals for that group and continue to strategize about other groups. School communities should also look at national data, especially in high schools where students are soon going to be competing with graduates from other districts. In short, accepting responsibility means understanding that the job is never done.

2. "Push" High Achievement

Clear expectations and demanding assessments create push for high achievement.

A Conversation with a Commuter Train Conductor

Conductor: What do you do?

Passenger: I work in education.

Conductor: I can tell by what you're reading. You know, when I go home at night I walk in the door, take off my coat and then check on my girls and make sure they are doing their homework. My wife and I, we believe that education is the way to liberation . . . yes, education is the way to liberation. I'm on the school board in Jersey, and you know, I figured it out. A failing school means a failing principal. That's what happens every time. (author's conversation on train)

By holding clear expectations embedded within rigorous measures of achievement, states across the nation are addressing the problems of differentiated expectations. Clear standards set universal goals for high achievement, while assessment systems define the levels of performance necessary to be considered high achievement. By clarifying both the "what" and the "how well," states are both assisting teachers in holding high expectations and demanding improved quality in teaching. Thus, rigorous systems of clear standards and demanding assessments help reverse the downdraft of low expectations that flood our secondary schools. There is support for teachers, administrators, schools, and districts to take on the societal forces of social reproduction and demand high achievement for all—the power of push.

Secondary schools that take push seriously will make extra effort to communicate how standards and assessments affect students' opportunities and access to postsecondary education. As soon as high school students enter the high school arena, they must meet expectations both in coursework and on high stakes exams. High school students face, for example, state assessments, exit exams, college admissions exams, placement tests, workplace tests, AP or IB exams, and in some cases portfolio requirements. High school faculty and the school's external community should help students understand what they must do, and what expectations are involved in each case. From the first day of high school, everything a student does matters in ways it hasn't before; this is a very new experience for 14- or 15-year-old students. At the end of their four years in high school, their GPA weighs in heavily in determining the choices they can make for college and work.

One of the keys to creating push is setting the expectation for hard work, or, as described in research, "effort-based learning" (Resnick 2000). Students need to understand that it is hard work that results in learning, not some innate intelligence or genetic code. High schools need to provide the supports and conditions for hard work, whether it's a homework hotline or more time within courses and throughout the high school sequence. Push probably means rethinking how students move through the high school sequence, including promotion practices and report cards. For example, schools may need to extend time within courses by "wrapping" summer months around the usual calendar to give some students more time inside the course. Under this scenario, some students might be enrolled in Algebra II for nine months while others for eleven months and still others for thirteen months.

Great attention has been paid to the power of holding high expectations and demanding high performance—the power of push. Public demands for improvement, the pressure of school choice, and the reality of large-scale accountability systems combine, among other things, to focus extensive attention on demanding teacher improvement. Exit exams, limits on social promotion, college entrance requirements, and other demands press high school students to perform, despite the reality that students can exit the system if the pressure is too great and the rewards too low.

3. "Pull" High Achievement

Putting achievement in context creates pull for high achievement. While push is a powerful force, the research informs us of another companion resource that can move mountains—the power of pull. This concept of using pull as a source of systemic power that dovetails with demand has received less attention, despite the preponderance of evidence that emerged from analysis of the secondary research literature. The research tells us loud and clear that context, the set of conditions and circumstances that envelop teaching and learning, is a powerful force available to impact quality secondary teaching and effective learning. The literature on student and teacher motivation systems supports the possibilities of improving both effort and achievement by aligning the school system demands with motivation systems that move people young and old to engage. Once high schools see more clearly the dynamics that are pressing on teachers and students, they can also see the potential for improving teaching and learning by changing the context in which teaching and learning occur. For example, teachers' sense of importance can be nurtured by a strong, supportive and demanding intellectual community, and thus, the context in which teachers work can positively impact teacher engagement by buffering the school community from the dynamics of social reproduction, among other things.

Students, too, are affected by context. Students engage in learning when school fits their own personal motivation systems—when they believe achieving in school is important, and when they believe achievement will move them toward a better personal future. Thus, schools and teachers can engage students by placing achievement opportunities and demands in context of students' motivation to learn. Students can be motivated to learn by increasingly placing school achievement in context of their future goals and aspirations, as well as by using the power inherent in their current belief system about what's important. By being more strategic and seeing education through the eyes of their students, schools can adjust the context so they increasingly drive high expectations for all. In short, pulling students to achieve by contextualizing expectations offers tremendous opportunity to increase student achievement.

Opportunities abound to move students as well as teachers toward improved performance through the power of attraction. When high schools and teachers provide the rationale for learning by nesting classroom demands in context of student motivation, they offer tantalizing possibilities for increasing student engagement inside the challenging work of learning at high levels. Let's now move on to the final conversation—looking more specifically at ideas for changing the dynamics of holding high expectations to updraft for all.

BOLD, BOLDER, BOLDEST!

The effort to recognize in our own districts and schools how the updraft/downdraft plays out brings us to a point of no return. Both good conscience and professional commitment require us to take action once we know that students are experiencing their secondary education with different expectations. To redirect class and racial stratification, the educational institution must gather will and create experiences to channel its forces into crafting equitable opportunities for all students. The optimistic position takes the view that once schools or districts have made sense of their analysis of school artifacts, they are positioned to contribute to the future of high school improvement. This means taking action on some level, whether it be small steps that involve making adjustments to the existing reality or challenging larger realities and impediments to reform. Though some districts or schools might find it possible to take at first only bold steps, making small changes within the existing system, others may be able to take bolder steps. Ultimately, though, the institution must strive for the boldest actions. It is here that high expectations for academic success operate for all students. Obviously, the realities of school and district life affect how daring actions can be; nevertheless, this section is meant to allow us to gaze at the horizon and dream. Of course, high school reform, like any reform, should not just take place for the sake of change. In fact, bold, bolder, boldest thinking involves combining the old with the new in meaningful ways.

The goal of this thinking is an education that prepares all students to have the opportunity to continue into postsecondary education, with a focus on what that means specifically for adolescents. Business has made it clear that workers will need the added value and experiences that postsecondary education offers. And, the political and social complexity of our twenty-first century lives demands that we extend our education into the postsecondary years to be prepared as adults and citizens. There are many ways to be bold, bolder and boldest. Our hope is that we stimulate your thinking and embolden your will to act.

The criterion for "bold" is that such actions can be done now without seeking changes in policy or major support from school boards, community or unions. Bold, of course, requires effort and time, so we are not saying it is easy. Bold, as does bolder and boldest, needs leadership from within the school and at different levels outside the school. "Bolder" pushes us to think beyond the current school climate and structures. "Boldest" calls for both community and schools to enact the major changes necessary to move more and more students into the updraft.

In this section we enlarge our vision of what high schools can become by including the visions of people involved in education or keenly invested in the progress of the American high school. Their descriptions should encourage us to imagine and act at the same time as we work to improve this educational and cultural institution that is at once real and ideal—high school.

BOLD

Bold starts with looking closely at what is happening, or not, inside our own high schools using the artifact analysis. Then, bold does something about the downdraft now, even if it means small steps or mid-year actions. Bold makes student achievement data and other artifact data and information public so that collective effort can be mustered to take on specific problems.

Bold addresses infrastructures that impede teacher effectiveness. For example, bold considers student/teacher ratios and who's teaching whom. Bold effectively uses schedules, team teaching, and other now well known strategies. For example, Bold adjusts the schedule to create two hours a day for teachers to meet because effective teaching depends on intensive training. Bold creates and recreates teams to provide the mix of expertise necessary to meet specific problem/solutions.

Bold monitors quality teaching to ensure that all coursework reflects high expectations for learning. Teachers review student work as data about effective teaching and share effective strategies. All staff take on the responsibility to prepare students for high-stakes assessments and college entrance requirements. Bold is evident when the teaching community monitors itself and demands quality teaching from everyone, using coaching and supervisory evaluations to communicate those expectations.

Bold means making sure supports really work for students, such as after-school programs, and integrates them into the goal of improving student achievement. Supports for students might include providing learning choices and other ways to engage and personalize the learning environment.

Bold thoughtfully adopts curricular programs working in other places to ratchet up the rigor in the curriculum as well as the level of expertise. This is a good choice when a school or district has high teacher turnover, for example. Schools have used a variety of packaged curriculums to create a core experience for all students. Schools use these "packaged" curriculums or programs to insert and maintain high demand and high support into curriculum and instruction.

Bold means building the intellectual and pedagogical capacity of the teaching force so that teachers are enabled to deliver rigorous and challenging curriculum. Providing graduate credit courses in content areas on high school campuses is an example of how districts can help teachers meet re-certification and professional development requirements while addressing the quality of teaching.

Bold brings elementary, middle school and high school teachers together to establish and understand what is happening up and down the continuum. High school and local colleges and other postsecondary institutions also meet regularly to build an understanding of the curricular continuum and expectations along the continuum.

BOLDER

Bolder thinking goes farther. It requires both institutional clout and community support to pull off, but it may mean the difference between moving the institution from making some gains to making substantial gains in improving all students' academic achievement. This level of action demands leadership throughout the system, from the superintendent to the teacher. It also asks for commitment coupled with patience. In some cases it might also ask to seek funding or use budgets differently.

Bolder uses resources so that the bottom line is effective teaching and learning. Analyzing how budgets support goals means making hard choices about what matters financially and educationally. For example, contracting out some aspects of the curriculum to local vendors, such as PE to the YMCA or math to the university, might free up needed funds for targeted areas. It means making bus schedules work for students' scheduling needs and not for organizational ones. For instance, students who must move during the school year within district could use the bus system to remain at their current site.

Bolder is willing to cut out what detracts and derails us from delivering a rigorous, interesting education to all students. It may mean we do not offer large numbers of courses or try to address areas beyond a core curriculum. Central Park East High School in New York made this commitment when the school eliminated PE and the arts, then contracted out these non-core subjects. Eliminating inefficient infrastructures when they are detected in order to create better working conditions for teaching and learning requires a large amount of "boldness" rather than waiting several months for summer until it's easier. That might mean changing schedules and staff arrangements mid-year, for example. The willingness to make such changes means that students will get what they need sooner rather than later. In high school, struggling students have no more time to wait or to stall. Four years is precious little time to make up for eleven years of not having been taught.

Bolder crafts the school day to achieve time and opportunity in those subjects that are assessed by the state (literacy, math, science and social studies) and postsecondary institutions (the same). This may mean going for waivers from state requirements, such as family consumer science and drivers' education, that take away from essential time on task in core subjects. (At least one state requires high school students to receive credits in nineteen areas.) It may also mean yearlong schedules or extended days.

Bolder reshapes the way students move and interact within a high school to create more personalization and attention—just what students say helps them push their learning. Mini-schools and learning choices allow for more personalized experiences for students and teachers alike. In one district, a school appropriately called School Without Walls operates out of a university and uses the city as it campus. The "middle college" is taking hold in a few districts and is blurring the distinction between high school and college as juniors and seniors move onto community college campuses.

Bolder looks at time not as a given but as flexible resource. England offers us an example of using "social capital accounts" to stretch time-on-task into the everyday lives of students. There, the school system provides tuition dollars to poor parents to send their students to music lessons, science camps, and other enrichment opportunities accessible to more affluent students.

Bolder considers the development of teachers and expertise as essential and dares to move beyond the traditional definitions of "teacher" to include people with knowledge and skills inside the larger community as resources and teaching partners.

Using standards-based report cards to communicate student performance requires bolder action. Because postsecondary institutions want class rank, A–F grades or percentile, high schools find it hard to use a standards-based grading system. Parents and community, unused to standards-based language, also pressure schools to continue using the vestiges of the bell-curve system.

BOLDEST

Until school and society are bound together by common purposes the program of education will lack both meaning and vitality.
—George S. Counts 1932

Boldest is clear about challenging and reshaping the social order by affirming all students access to future educational opportunities. And, paradoxically, boldest actions are the most likely to be sustained because they reach deep into the high school and demand support from all constituents. Ultimately, this commitment protects it from the forays of interest groups and public school nay-sayers. This is why boldest visions are talked and written about, though seemingly impossible, because of political or social impediments. As a result, reinventing the high school is more often the stuff of conferences and articles. If, however, educators and communities could come to understand that most of these objections have more to do with adults than with students, perhaps these misgivings could be dismissed as irrelevant. Then, the institution would be freed to take strides toward reinventing the high school in ways that honor all students. At the base of boldest is the belief that our society realizes its democracy though a community of learners who reflect our society and all its diversity. We become more capable, competent, inventive, creative, invigorated, enthu-

Social Survival

When a school is established, it is a clear indication that the group sponsoring the school means to perpetuate itself by providing its children in a systematized way with the knowledge and values it deems necessary for survival. (Gutek 1970)

siastic, knowledgeable and responsible citizenry when we educate all our children well.

Boldest creates designs that fuse the transition between high school and college in such a way that there is no transition. It could mean a high school that has developed a seamless curriculum so that graduating from high school means admissions to college. This would leave open the possibility of redesigning the K–16 system into different chunks to meet the needs of the contemporary lifestyle and curriculum. Some have suggested schools be broken down into smaller groupings: P–3, 4–7, 8–10, 11–12 and post-secondary. Some have suggested fewer groupings: P–8, 9–12 and post-secondary or P–10 and 11–16.

Boldest means flexible matriculation whereby students move through high school at their own pace. This system requires rethinking time and designing a series of pre and post exams, portfolios and other curricular tools to mark mastery of standards and coursework. Technology is already emerging as a tool for making a flexible system possible in high schools as it already is in cyber-universities. Boldest of the bold might actually eliminate high school, as it exists, for those students who learn best in the world outside of school by aligning standards to "on-the-job" work. For example, in a physics lab or newspaper office, students would complete their high school curricula on the job in the workplace or through apprenticeships. This would mean moving all or part of the learning experience outside the context of courses and classrooms altogether. Boldest also demystifies the workplace, integrating the community and business in ways that are already established in Germany and France. By aligning workplace activities and jobs to standards in rigorous and meaningful terms, business can become co-teachers in high school.

Boldest fuses personal life choices with school through the use of cyber courses and mentoring sites. By combining tutorials with electronic schools, districts can reach out to students whose lives make it impossible to be on campus. A student might complete work at home or at another site and check in periodically with a mentor-teacher and other off-site students.

Perhaps, some of the boldest ideas circulating in education conversations involve changes in the teaching profession. These include: certification offered by school districts so that districts can better control what new teachers bring into the system; year-long contracts; business and other professionals entering the system on leave and teachers entering the "real world" for a time to gain new experiences; and merit-pay based on student achievement. Some of these ideas are in the works and will probably become merely bold in the future.

Bold, bolder, boldest each plot a course for reinventing the middle and high school experiences. However, if we are truly to create more equitable educational experiences for both advantaged and disadvantaged students in the twenty-first century, then we must move as quickly as possible to boldest. It is there that standards-based education realizes the democracy of "equity and excellence" so often cited in our public documents and education laws and policies. Because such a goal is so demanding and yet so vital to the lives of adolescents and young adults, it will take all of us to unleash the full potential of boldest thinking and acting.

The shift from schools that are working for some students to those that work for all students takes time, energy and talent as well as resources and support from within and from without the schools. Ultimately, it takes constant monitoring to sustain the good work each generation of teachers, administrators and community contribute toward a truly equitable education for its children. Secondary schools serve to refine and deepen the knowledge and skills young students learn in the earlier years and to position the adolescent for adult life. Because high school plays this important role in our students' lives, we must continue to question how the system serves students. By looking around us, on our desks, in our classrooms and inside our common documents, we believe schools can find the data and information they need to take bold, bolder and boldest actions. *Updraft/Downdraft* evolved from our own desire to better understand if what seemed so intractable about secondary schooling really was or if there was something we could do to unleash the hidden powers within the human, material, fiscal and temporal resources buried inside middle and high schools. Our hope is that school and community leadership will act on the public challenge to graduate students who will make our society productive and proud, instead of "hammering on cold iron."

Epilogue: Noah's Beauty

*Terry Roberts and Laura Billings,[1] Directors
National Paideia Center, Greensboro, NC*

Imagine this scene in a high school classroom. A large urban high school in Southern California. The autumn of 2004.

There are 32 juniors and seniors sitting in a loosely formed hollow square. In the group are 17 girls and 15 boys. Some are athletes and cheer-leaders; some punks and gothic, all with skin more-or-less brown or black, pink, or pale white. Some are native speakers of Spanish, Portuguese, French, various dialects of English, and one tribal dialect of Vietnamese so rare that it doesn't have a name in America. In this group are personal names as diverse as Ramone and Susan, Vientura and Ben, Chevrolet and Eddie, Huang Lu and Noah.

These 32 are in a Social Studies classroom. They have met for the third of six annual capstone seminars at Jerry Brown High School. A capstone seminar is a schoolwide event designed to address the stunningly diverse and troubled community that is their school. That is almost any high school in twenty-first century America.

The capstone seminar at Jerry Brown is intended to build bridges of many kinds: bridges between students and their teachers; between older and younger students; and perhaps most important of all—between students separated by gender, race, creed, language, clique, and stereotype. Bridges between human beings and the web of ideas that the human community has created. These ideas—social and cultural concepts—can sometimes serve to bind diverse people together. Can sometimes become the connective tissue that joins these fragile humans in the face of the vicious forces that would tear them apart and pit them against each other.

---

1. Terry Roberts is director of the National Paideia Center. Laura Billings is associate director.

For some ideas—justice, democracy, faith, family, freedom, peace, hope, love, the doing unto others as you would have done unto you—are so powerful in their working out that they are capable of defining a generation of young people, requiring of them dedication, belief, devotion to something larger than themselves. The theme for this year's capstone series, for example, is the Latin phrase *e pluribus unum*—"out of many one"—and as always when planning seminars, the seminar committee had struggled to find texts rich in ideas.

These 32 are not unlike thousands of other students. And this classroom is not unlike scores of other classrooms across America where teachers are using the ancient ritual of democratic discourse to unlock their students. Unlock them to ideas and to each other.

The leader of this seminar is a middle-aged black woman. A veteran Social Studies teacher named Naomi Ben-Ami who has learned through several years of practice how to open up the minds of her students through subtle and open-ended questioning. She is widely admired by her students despite the fact that she is demanding and somewhat mysterious—as well as serene and caring while passionate about the study of history.

The text for this year's third capstone seminar is, of all things, an ancient French Fairy Tale: "La Belle et Le Bete" ["Beauty and the Beast"]. Not, as the students have come to understand, the sugary Walt Disney version, but the much older, much darker, much more ambiguous tale that evolved through years of European retelling. After all, the great tales of folk tradition are inherently classical. That is, they have not only survived through the generations before they were written down; they have by selective listening and even more selective retelling added layer upon layer of meaning until they have become beautifully complex knots of individual and group psychology.

For a week, the English and Social Studies departments had woven folk tales and folklore, legends and songs into their curricula. The French department had staged a reading of "La Belle et Le Bete" in French for elementary students; and the film class had held a showing of Jean Cocteau's classic 1946 film version of the tale. The story in its myriad versions was in the air.

But now, as Naomi Ben-Ami knew, the time had come to ask them to think. And in a way she had been both anticipating and dreading it. Although the seminar was the culmination of a well-thought out succession of events, it was difficult to bring off in the highly charged atmosphere of an urban high school. All the fear and distrust, anger and resentment that lay just beneath the surface of the adolescent psyche could surface when students were asked to discuss candidly what they actually thought and felt about the human condition. In fact, the rules of the seminar, as Naomi was now carefully reminding her 32, were explicitly designed to help participants disagree gracefully and without rancor.

The previous year schoolwide seminars at Jerry Brown had almost been suspended when a fight had broken out during a discussion of Martin Luther King's "I Have a Dream" speech. The irony of this—what was almost a riot fueled by King's impassioned call for non-violent social change—was not lost on the Brown faculty, but still many were afraid. Afraid they admitted, of honesty, of openness, of students thinking outloud in a public forum. But the capstone seminar series survived when student representatives on the seminar committee argued that the single fight was a symptom, not the disease proper, and that the fight along with the discussion that followed, probably prevented much more violence than it ever could have caused. So the seminar as a schoolwide event survived. And so Naomi Ben-Ami came to ask her opening question.

She had seated male and female students alternately in her seminar circle, as well as juniors with seniors, so that for the initial question, students were mostly paired with someone of the opposite gender and with someone a year older or younger. Someone who, in many instances, was all but a stranger.

"With your partner," Ben-Ami began, "discuss a response to this question. Pick either Beauty or the Beast: what is one important thing she—or he—learned from the other? In a moment, we'll go round the circle and a spokesperson from each pair will share your initial response. Now, one more time . . ." As she repeated the prompt, Ben-Ami watched to see which pairs seemed most uncomfortable with each other. Those, she knew, she'd have to coach a bit.

Ben-Ami sat on the school seminar committee and had helped choose this text over the protests of those who argued that students wouldn't take it seriously. She knew that the vast majority of students were used to at least one seminar a week in some academic course and that they would begin the process in good faith. It was up to her questions to open the doors of the text so that they became interested and excited about the treasures within.

As she had been trained to do after asking a paired question, she got up and walked around the inside of the hollow square, auditing each group to see if they were talking openly to each other, checking to see if they were close to resolution. One pair, a boy Ben-Ami had taught the year before and a girl he obviously knew—were chatting happily in Spanish, she waving the text at him for emphasis. She signaled them to talk only more quietly. Two of the pairs eyed each other distrustfully and pretended to read to avoid conversation. She knelt and coached, drawing them out with specific questions about the woman and the animal in the tale.

Then she came to Chevrolet and Noah. Chevrolet was a loud, fun-loving nineteen year old woman who was finally (as she herself said) a senior. After a wild and bumpy ride through the first two years of high school, she'd settled down and applied herself. She still showed up in a Harley-Davidson T-shirt on occasion, in part Ben-Ami believed, because her father had died in a bike wreck, in part because it was invariably the only one in a school of 2,500 students. From her journal, Ben-Ami knew she sported the tattoo of a sun flower where it couldn't be seen, a slight indiscretion in ink that she was alternately proud and ashamed of.

Chevrolet was talking excitedly in a stage-whisper into Noah's ear. Noah was a 16-year-old junior, legitimately shy, Ben-Ami decided after a moment's observation. He was nodding rhythmically to Chevrolet's monologue, probably in self-defense as much as agreement. Ben-Ami watched curiously for almost a minute before moving on. Noah was the kind of student teachers of her generation had been trained to watch for. He was dressed entirely in black, even his hair (brown at the roots) died the color of a raven's wing. She'd noticed him in the halls, always alone, often twisted into a corner reading. Young for his age, tender almost beneath the hard attitude he'd assumed. And by chance, he'd been paired with a girl twenty years older in experience.

Ben-Ami sat back down and continued her instructions. "I want each pair to choose a spokesperson to share your thoughts with the group. One minute per group. Put your heads together and a few minutes we'll begin." She finished filling in her seating chart so that once the actual seminar began, she could focus on tallying responses and noting ideas. After a moment it was clear that most of the groups were ready and she let the first spokesperson begin—the Spanish speaking girl who had been so excited a moment before and who now waved her arm to volunteer.

"Weelllllll, Caesar and I, we think that it is very important that the monster learned to speak. I mean learned to speak the language of the girl. Belle. He had lived in that country for a long time, we think, but at the beginning of the story, he only said a few short words and than a lot of grunts and growls and howls." [LAUGHTER] "Lots of howling at night . . . So until he began to fall in love with Belle, he had no reason to learn her language. But then . . ." Caesar's partner, whose name Naomi realized from her seating chart was Rachel, rolled her eyes expressively. Naomi jotted down "love = language" beside Rachel's name in the circle and shifted her attention to the next pair.

"She . . . Belle, I mean, learned to look past the surface. When she first saw him, she saw a (the spokesperson, boy this time, glanced at his text) 'ravening beast' but eventually she looked past all the exterior and began to see what was inside him. But you know, she tried to run away in the beginning despite her vow. Because as good a person as she was, she still couldn't see past the surface. That came later."

"She was a child in the beginning, but she was more like a woman at the end." This from a young woman who, Naomi knew, was finishing high school that year despite having a child—four years old—of her own. "In the beginning, she was so idealistic and self- . . . " to her partner, "What was the word?" He whispered to her, "Self-righteous . . ." "So self-right-eous that she thought she was throwing herself away to save her father like some kind of saint. It was only when she had to nurse the Beast when he was hurt and when she had to be tender and kind—really kind, not just kind out of a book—that she began to grow up." Naomi drew a line from this young woman's name (Vientura) in her seating chart to a box on the page she saved for later questions and wrote: "What's the difference between being really kind and kind like in a book?"

In the next pair, the girl, a junior, was pushing her partner, a senior boy, to speak. She black, he white. He a rough kid with a tattoo of thorns around his biceps. A football player who had been expelled at least once the previous spring for fighting. And yet, Naomi knew, a young man who, according to a colleague, could write well and should go on to college. "You tell it," she said loud enough for everyone to hear, "it's your idea."

He blushed the color of his hair—crew-cut red. "I think it's simple, really.
He had to learn to control his temper. Trust me, I know how hard that is
to do, and until he learned that, he couldn't understand her and he could-
n't let her close enough to understand him." "Understanding = is it important?" Naomi wrote.

The next pair in the circle was Chevrolet and Noah. She was obviously
anxious to speak, but actually seemed unsure of what to say, completely
uncharacteristic for her. Noah was scribbling furiously in the margins of
his text with the nub of a pencil. Naomi started to correct him for not paying attention, but then realized he was writing Chevrolet a note. Chevrolet glanced down and then began, continuing to look down as she went.
"Me and Noah haven't quite got this all worked out, but Noah says . . . I
mean we say . . . being in love makes you more awake to the entire world.
It makes you able to learn. See, the one thing that would save the Beast
(Chevrolet was gaining momentum) was both learning to love and being
worthy of love." She glanced down at a word her partner was pointing to
emphatically. "According to the text, he had to both learn to love and he
had to inspire love in another." Chevrolet heaved a sigh of relief as if she
had arrived at the end of a recitation. Noah, who had not looked up from
his desk except to glance sideways at Chevrolet, was nodding in support.
Nodding and blushing.

Naomi was startled out of the reticence she usually practiced during the
opening round of a seminar. "Noah, are you saying that love somehow
equals learning?" She immediately wished she hadn't honored their response more than the others, that she'd had the self-control to wait to ask
that question.

Noah replied, but so softly that no one except Chevrolet could hear him.
"What we are saying," Chevrolet said, "is that that an strong sense of another person, or animal in this case, and an intense sense of the world
around you both inspire learning. About everything." Naomi wondered if
the girl had any sense of what she'd just translated. Wondered if she herself did. "We'll come back to your ideas," Naomi said aloud. "Along with
everyone else's . . . Next group." She wrote "does love = learning?" next
to Noah's name.

Naomi Ben-Ami managed to hold to the design of the original question—having each pair's spokesperson reply briefly—all the way round
the group before she let the discussion open up so that any participant

could reply at will. As soon as the last spokesperson in the circle had offered an initial contribution, the discussion took off of its own accord, the focus of most comments being what either Belle or the Beast learned from each other. Naomi listened carefully while at the same time marking a tally beside each student's name when she or he offered a comment, all the while taking notes in the margin of her seating chart.

In the previous five years, Naomi had led dozens upon dozens of seminars, both in her regular classes and in schoolwide events like this one. She had developed the habit of timing herself between questions, disciplining herself both in terms of wait time (the amount of silence she allowed after she asked a question) and to limit her own participation in the discussion to a bare and elegant minimum. In other words, she wanted to insert just enough teacher talk to keep the conversation engaged with the ideas inherent to the text. After approximately eight minutes of increasingly participatory discussion (and after six of the boys and eight of the girls had participated voluntarily), she inserted her first core question. "Sarah said a moment ago—and most of you seemed to agree—that neither Belle nor the Beast learned much in the beginning. Their learning came later in the story. Assuming you agree with Sarah, why do you think that was the case?"

Almost before the words were out of her mouth, Ramone, a startlingly handsome young black man, spoke. "She had to overcome her prejudice. In the beginning, she couldn't learn anything from him because she thought he was less than human. [Other students around the circle were nodding, some emphatically!] It's like when a black guy dates a white girl. I don't care what you say, in the beginning, she don't think he's like her." Caught up in his comment, Naomi began to ask a follow-up question, but was cut off by several students speaking at once. Finally, one gained the floor, Chevrolet, leaning so far forward she almost tipped over her desk. "Ramone, what about the Beast? Didn't he have to overcome his prejudice?"

"I don't think so," Ramone said. "Not in the same way."

"I think they both had prejudice. I think they both had prejudice. I think they both had prejudice." Huang Lu, an outgoing Asian boy was saying his one sentence over and over until he had everyone's attention. Most of the students laughed. He wanted to be an actor and they were used to his speeches.

"Yes, Huang, how would that be?" Chevrolet offered the invitation.

"I think that in the beginning of the tale, both Belle and the Beast wanted to use the other for something. She wanted to use him to bring some kind of fantasy and magic into her life, like Ms. Ben-Ami said the other day, some exotic into her dull life. She wanted to tame the wild beast. He wanted to use her to break the spell he was under. And this is important because anytime you want to use someone else for your own purposes, they become less human to you. And to me that is the nature of prejudice. You don't see the person, you see the type. White, black. Male, female. Animal, human. Doesn't matter."

Naomi scribbled a question on a note card and slipped it to the girl beside her to ask, a habit she'd developed for engaging very shy students in the conversation. The girl, Rosetta, read it aloud quietly and then again, more loudly. "Why is the Beast an animal rather than some other type of human?"

After a moment, Susan, an Honors student in English and Social Studies, but a girl the others teased about being so naive, spoke up. "Is it that the author is trying to say that we are all part spirit and part animal? Like in the Renaissance, the Great Chain of Being?" Several students laughed derisively at such a blatantly academic reference.

Naomi avoided answering her question by deflecting it to the group. "Hey, I agree with Susan," Ramone said. "It's the conflict between our animal nature and our higher, more spiritual nature." Chevrolet growled like a big cat; most of the students laughed; and Susan blushed.

"Are you making fun of Susan, Chevrolet?" Ben-Ami asked.

"Oh no, I'm agreeing with her," Chevrolet said and growled again. Even Susan laughed this time.

"But the real question about this animal thing," a participant's voice broke through the laughter, "is why is the animal, the Beast, a man, and the more human character a woman?" It was Gabrielle, a junior who was famous in Ben-Ami's class for her feminist views. And as Ben-Ami knew from her journal, was an even angrier young woman than the rest of the students realized.

The laughter ended abruptly and there was a sudden pregnant pause. Ben-Ami let the silence grow as she watched the group. She wondered who would take on the question—and at the same time run the risk of taking on Gabrielle. She noticed Noah scribbling furiously with Chevrolet reading over his shoulder. The silence stretched uncomfortably (actually less than ten seconds by Ben-Ami's watch) until Ramone (of course, Ben-Ami thought) spoke. "Cause there is this stereotype, Gabrielle, that men are more violent, more aggressive, more insensitive, less thoughtful, less spiritual, less caring."

He paused to breathe, and Gabrielle seized the moment. "Less collaborative, less caring for the group, more violent."

Chevrolet held out her hand to signal that she wanted to insert a word before Ramone could reply. "Noah says that in the beginning of the story, the Beast is a symbol for the male ego." Noah nudged her and pointed at what he'd written, but before Chevrolet could continue, Ben-Ami said, "Let him speak for himself, Chevrolet. Noah, what did you write?"

Noah whispered and Chevrolet repeated, "The Beast is a huge male ego with fur." Gabrielle nodded emphatically at Chevrolet, ignoring Noah.

"Wait, wait, wait a minute." Vientura, a thin, usually reticent black girl—woman really, working two jobs while she struggled to finish school. "I just have to say this. The seminar is the place where you s'posed to speak the truth, right?" Ben-Ami nodded. "Well, when I began reading this, I figured what this was all about was that the Beast represented black people and the pretty little girl that thought she was so damn smart represented white people. I admit, Gabrielle, that for a while I thought it was a black boy, white girl thing—don't start, Ramone, you know what I'm talking about—but when I got here today, I thought it was all about race. White people who don't think black people are human, at least not as human as they are."

A dozen participants began speaking at once, but Vientura held the floor without Ben-Ami's help. "Ya'all listen to me. I'm not finished. Listen! After sitting here and listening to ya'all go on for 30 minutes, I think it's bigger than that. This is hard for me to explain, but I think it's about all the different things that separate people. I don't mean people in general. I mean whatever separates two people that need each other, that could help and understand each other. That could accept each other."

There was another long pause in the discussion, and a glance at her notes showed Ben-Ami that only 20 of the 32 participants had taken a talk turn after the initial round-robin opening, of those 20, perhaps six had dominated the discussion so far. Based on this assessment, she shaped her next question: "I want to bring us back to the text. I've heard a lot of comments about what separated the two (Beauty and Beast) in the beginning of the tale, and my next question is based on what I've heard you say so far. I want the original pairs to examine the tale itself to see what kinds of things actually brought them together . . . . Then the other person in the pair will act as spokesperson."

After she repeated the directions and the pairs began to stage whisper together, Ben-Ami circled each name on her seating chart that hadn't yet spoken to the entire group. Part of her personal agenda was to teach the active use of each student's own voice, and she was passionate about that facet of the seminar—passionate but, she hoped, subtle. Thus the technique of asking the students to first discuss in pairs and then have the more introverted of the two act as spokesperson. This time as the groups discussed she remained seated, but she did carefully "walk" her eyes around the circle, studying each group in turn. She smiled to see Chevrolet coaching Noah, apparently making him write down what he wanted to say . . . or perhaps what she wanted him to say.

This time when they started the paired responses, Rachel volunteered again, and even tried to speak for Caesar until Ben-Ami made it clear that it was the silent partner's turn.

Caesar: "remember how we say that the Beast learn Belle's language. Learn to speak. How love is learning to speak. We have developed our idea some more. It is also her that learn his language. When she learns to feed the animals with him. When she learns to growl at the cat to scare it away from the birds."

There was a pause and from across the circle, Drenna (who hadn't yet spoken) said, "Caesar, may I ask a question?" Caesar nodded; Naomi nodded to encourage her. "Do you mean that they both have to learn the other's language? . . . Because it hurts to have to lose your own language (suddenly Naomi heard just the faintest accent in Drenna's speech) when you're forced to learn another."

Caesar looked down at his desk—perhaps in pain—but Rachel nodded. "Yes, where does my Spanish go when I learn to speak English in this country? In this school?"

Drenna: "I understand, Rachel. I no longer can talk to my grandmother in Portuguese. And so how am I to know who I am?"

It was as if someone had thrown gasoline on a smoldering fire. Suddenly ten students tried to speak at once—in (Naomi calculated later) at least five languages. Caesar was nodding emphatically, his eyes closed in the ecstasy of the idea. Rachel, his partner, was waving her arms to get everyone's attention and pointing at Huang Lu on the other side of the circle. "Let him," she finally shouted, "let him tell it."

In his textbook English, the young Japanese American said, "To lose one's language in a new and different culture is to lose one's past, to lose one's childhood, to lose what makes one."

"Unique." Someone close on Naomi's left said the word. Most of the students in the circle looked at her in surprise, and she realized that Eric had spoken. Eric, who she always placed beside her in the seminar circle. Eric, who was her worst discipline problem. Eric, who rarely ever spoke in class except in hip-hop rhymes.

Hiding his surprise, Huang Lu asked, "What did you say, Eric?"

Eric looked up and met Huang Lu's gaze. "I said unique. It ain't just if your language is some other language. I speak American, but I rap. And when I come in here, she . . ." Eric nodded roughly toward Naomi. "tries to make me speak the standard. She's robbing what makes me unique. Or what make you . . . or you . . . or you . . . or any of you unique. She makes you bleeeend."

Naomi stifled the almost overwhelming urge to defend herself.

"Ms. Ben-Ami?" It was Susan trying to get her attention.

"Yes?"

"We know you want to go round the circle and get everybody to speak. If we all agree to talk, can we just explore this a little? Can't we just go back to plain talking?"

Naomi glanced around the circle to see a number of heads nodding and quickly checked her seating chart. "If I can hear from . . . Lynelle . . . and Brian . . . and Noah during the next fifteen minutes, then I'm more than happy if we keep on going. But . . ." She raised her hand for emphasis. "I also want us to return to the text. In the end of the tale, the Beast has learned Belle's language and, according to Caesar, she has also learned some of his. Have they lost more than they've gained by learning this new language, by this blending they've gone through? Is that what some of you are saying?"

"I think that blending is not such a bad thing if it's your choice." This from Brian, one of the three who hadn't spoken since the beginning. "I mean, she is held captive there, sort of like we're held captive here

[SOME LAUGHTER], but they both choose to learn the other's ways, the other's language."

"And the Beast does let her go," Gabrielle added. "As hard as it is to believe, he lets her choose whether to stay away or come back, so she's not a prisoner at the end."

A.J. the football player: "I agree with Gabrielle. It's when the Beast let's her go, gives her the freedom to choose, that's the turning point between them."

Naomi, suddenly realizing how close they were to the end of the period, pushed forward the closing question that had been slowly forming in her mind for the last half of the discussion. "Let's look together at the last page. Next to the last paragraph. Where it reads 'and Beauty found the Beast stretched full length upon the ground.' Who would like to read from there to the end of the paragraph. Lynelle?"

Without looking up, the shyest girl in the class began. "Stretched full length upon the ground. Stretched beneath the maple tree where they had in the winter fed the smaller animals. He was, she saw clearly, dying, the great heart beating ever so slowly."

"Belle dove to the ground beside him where she could thrust her lips as close to his ear as possible. 'Beast, Beast,' she whispered. 'I love you. Don't die now. Don't die now that I know. I love you.' And his heart stopped beating. His huge chest became still. But kneeling on the other side of the Beast's body was a young man. A young man who reached over the Beast to take her hand. 'And I you,' he said."

Just as a few minutes ago, the seminar had seemed ready to explode, it now fell eerily silent. The shy 15-year-old girl had read the words so beautifully that they had taken on their ancient magic.

Naomi waited. Two, three, four, five seconds. And then whispered. "Who is transformed at this moment?" "He is," Ramone said at the same moment Susan said, "She is."

"Why?" Naomi followed, still whispering. "The ultimate seminar question: why?"

"He was willing to die for her freedom," Noah said quietly, gazing at Chevrolet, but in the ethereally quiet room, his words were audible. And when he realized the others were listening, he actually spoke up. "The man inside the Beast was actually willing to run the risk of dying for her to have her freedom. He was willing to give her what she needed no matter the cost."

"And that transformed him," Chevrolet had picked up the thread of Noah's thought. ". . . from the inside out. As if the man was growing up inside the Beast. And since he was growing, she had to grow in response. Oh, my God, I can see it. When she realized that she might have caused his death, she rushed back. And when she saw him lying on the ground, the woman who had been growing up inside her was born. She threw herself down on the ground beside him even though she was wearing a dress her father gave her." Naomi could see that Noah was entranced by his seminar partner—undergoing a transformation of his own, she suspected.

"So she was transformed too?" Susan asked.

"Oh yes," Chevrolet answered. "She only thought she was a woman before." Chevrolet glanced around the circle. "Like us."

"This is my final question," Naomi interjected into the pause. "Is this a fairy tale for children or for adults?"

"The beginning is for children," Noah said clearly. "The ending is for adults."

Bibliography

PROLOGUE: WHY NOT?

Traub, J. (April 2, 2002). "The Test Mess," *New York Times Magazine,* p. 60.

CHAPTER 1: "HAMMERING ON COLD IRON"

Bannon, L. (August 23, 2001). "What Happened When Well-to-do Parents Tried to Prep a Public School for Their Kids," *Wall Street Journal.*

Education Trust. (2000). *Achievement in America 2000.* Online at www.edtrust.org.

Hartcollins, A. (October 31, 2001). "Scarsdale Warned Not to Boycott State Tests." *New York Times* (in *Metropolitan Desk*).

Herbert, B. (September 3, 2001). "On the Way to Nowhere." *New York Times* (in *Opinion*).

Johnson, D. S. (November 11, 2001). "As Schools Adjust to Tests, Parental Anger Is Standard." *Washington Post,* p. C1.

Lewis, S. (1922). *Babbitt.* Online version at Bartleyby.com. Chapter 18.

National Commission on the High School Senior Year. (October 2001). *Raising Our Sights: No High School Senior Left Behind.* The Woodrow Wilson National Fellowship Foundation, p. 9.

Powell, M. (May 18, 2001). "In N.Y. Putting Down Their Pencils: Parent Rebellion against Standardized Testing Strikes at Heart of Bush Plan." *Washington Post,* p. A1.

Shulte, B., and Keating, D. (Series beginning August 31, 2001). "Pupil's Poverty Drives Achievement Gap." *Washington Post.*

Sedlak, M. W., Wheeler, C. W., Pullin, D. C., and Cusick, P. A. (1986). *Selling Students Short: Classroom Bargains and Academic Reform in the American High School.* New York: Teachers College Press, p. 48.

Traub, J. (April 2, 2002). "The Test Mess." *New York Times Magazine,* p. 60.

CHAPTER 2: UPDRAFT/DOWNDRAFT

Casserly, M. (January 24, 1996). "Commentary: Discipline and Demographics: The Problem Is Not Just the Kids." *Education Week.*

Cusick, P. A. (1983). *The Egalitarian Ideal and the American High School: Studies of Three Schools.* New York: Longman.

Education Trust. (2000). *Achievement in America 2000.* Online at www.edtrust.org.

Gladwell, M. (2000). *The Tipping Point: How Little Things Can Make a Big Difference.* New York: Little, Brown and Company, p. 140

Goodlad, J. I. (1984). *A Place Called School: Prospects for the Future.* New York: McGraw-Hill.

Lee, V. E., Smith, J. B., and Croninger, R. G. (1995). *Another Look at High School Restructuring: More Evidence That It Improves Student Achievement and More Insight into Why.* University of Wisconsin, Madison. Center on Organization and Restructuring of Schools.

MacLeod, J. (1995). *Ain't No Makin' It: Aspirations and Attainment in a Low-Income Neighborhood.* Boulder, CO: Westview Press.

McNeil, L. M. (1986). *Contradictions of Control: School Structure and School Knowledge.* New York: Routledge.

Metz, M. H. (1990). How social class differences shape teachers' work. In M. W. McLaughlin, J. E. Talbert, and N. Bascia (eds.), *The Contexts of Teaching in Secondary Schools: Teachers' Realities.* New York: Teachers College Press, pp. 40–107.

Metz, M. H. (1993). Teachers' Ultimate Dependence on Their Students. In J. W. Little and M. W. McLaughlin (eds.), *Teacher's Work: Individuals, Colleagues and Context.* New York: Teachers College Press, pp. 104–136.

Murphy, J. (2000). Conversation with author.

Murphy, J., Beck, L., Crawford, M. Hodges, A., and McGaughy, C. (2001). *The Productive High School: Creating Personalized Academic Communities.* Thousand Oaks, CA: Corwin Press.

Murphy, J., and Hallinger, P. (January 1985). "Effective High Schools: What are the Common Characteristics?" *NASSP Bulletin, 69*(477), pp. 18–22.

Nakao, A. (June 9, 1998). "Peer Power: Blacks 'Can't Just Drop Their Kids Off at School and Assume They'll Get the Same Education as Whites.'" *Examiner Staff,* from web site.

Newmann, F. M. (1985). *Educational Reform and Social Studies: Implications of Six Reports.* Boulder, CO: Social Science Education Consortium.

Oakes, J., and Lipton, M. (1996). Developing alternatives to tracking and grading. In L. I. Rendon, R. O. Hope, and Associates (eds.), *Educating a New Majority: Transforming America's Educational System for Diversity.* San Francisco: Jossey-Bass, pp. 168–200.

Oakes, J., Quartz, K. H., Ryan, S., and Lipton, M. (2000). *Becoming Good American Schools: The Struggle for Civic Virtue in Education Reform.* San Francisco: Jossey-Bass, p. 116.

Rutter, M., Maughan, B., Mortimore, P., and Ouston, J. (with Smith, A.). (1979). *Fifteen Thousand Hours: Secondary Schools and Their Effects on Children.* Cambridge, MA: Harvard University Press.

Sedlak, M. W., Wheeler, C. W., Pullin, D. C., and Cusick, P. A. (1986). *Selling Students Short: Classroom Bargains and Academic Reform in the American High School.* New York: Teachers College Press.

Steinberg, L. (with Brown, B. B., and Dornbusch, S. M.). (1996). *Beyond the Classroom: Why School Reform Has Failed and What Parents Need to Do.* New York: Teachers College Press.

CHAPTER 3: WHAT ARE ARTIFACTS AND WHY USE THEM?

Murphy, J., and Hallinger, P. (March-April 1989). "Equity as Access to Learning: Curricular and Instructional Treatment Differentials." *Journal of Curricular Studies, 21*(2), pp. 129–149.

CHAPTER 4: A HIGH SCHOOL CASE STUDY

Jones, O. (2001). Comment to author.
Sommerville, J. (2001). Comment to author.

CHAPTER 5: ANALYZING CALENDARS, STUDENT SCHEDULES, AND MASTER SCHEDULES

Haycock, K. (2001). Comment at presentation at NASH conference, Reno, NV.

128

Bibliography

CHAPTER 6: HOW TO ANALYZE
CURRICULUM AND INSTRUCTION

Adelman, C. (February/March 2001). *Tools for Schools*. National Staff Development Council.

Appleby, A. (2001). "Toward Thoughtful Curriculum: Fostering Disciplined-Based Conversation in the English Language Arts Classroom." Center on English Learning and Achievement (CELA) online report (1.10), p. 2.

Chall, J. (2000). *The Academic Challenge: What Really Works in the Classroom?* New York: Gilford Press, p. 171.

Dougherty, E. (2001). *Shifting Gears: Standards, Assessments, Curriculum and Instruction.* Golden, CO: Fulcrum Press.

Education Trust. (2000). *Achievement in America.* Online at www.edtrust.org. Includes slides from Sanders and Mendro.

Haberman, M. (1995). "Selecting 'Star' Teachers for Children and Youth in Urban Poverty." *Phi Delta Kappan, 76*(10), pp. 777–781.

Ardovino, J., Hollingsworth, J., and Ybarra, S. (2000). Multiple Measures: Accurate Ways to Assess Student Achievement. Thousand Oaks, CA: Corwin Press.

Lee, V. E., and Burkam, D. T. (December 18, 2000). "Dropouts in America: The Role of School Organization and Structure." Online. The Civil Rights Project, Harvard University.

Mitchell, R. (1998). *Front-End Alignment.* Golden, CO: Fulcrum Press.

National Commission on the High School Senior Year. (October 2001). *Raising Our Sights: No High School Senior Left Behind.* The Woodrow Wilson National Fellowship Foundation, p. 9.

Resnick, L. (2000). Presentation at the Education Trust National Conference, Washington, DC.

Trent Academy. Online at www.theschools.com.

Walker, V. S. (2000). "Valued Segregated Schools for African American Children in the South, 1935–1969: A Review of Common Themes and bCharacteristics." *Review of Education Research, 70*(3), pp. 264–267.

CHAPTER 7: CREATING UPDRAFT
FOR ALL—BOLD, BOLDER, BOLDEST!

Gutek, G. (1970). *An Historical Introduction to American Education.* New York: Thomas Y. Crowell Company, p. 9.

Appendix 1: Collecting Information

1. District Information

- Size
- Demographics
- Budget
- Category (urban, rural, etc.)
- Community demographics
- Centralization/decentralization of choices controlled by district versus choices controlled by school (i.e., specified district-wide programs versus school choice for programs such as math; governance)

2. Student Information

- Number of students in school
- Demographics (race/ethnicity; gender; socio-economic level; special education; ELL)
- Completion rates/dropout rates
- Attendance rates

3. Staff Information

- How administration, certified, and non-certified positions are allocated to schools, and who has choice in positions selected for each category
- Number of administrative, certified, and non-certified FTEs
- Teacher quality data (degree, years experience, certification, in field/out of field)

4. School Organization

- Kind of school (magnet, neighborhood, etc.)
- Teacher-student grouping infrastructure (SLCs, teams)
- Tracked/non-tracked status (overall and for different courses/programs)
- Available courses (number and types of courses)
- Master schedule including class cap sizes and student enrollment data for each course)
- Time infrastructure (block or regular schedule; number periods in schedule and length of periods; course lengths; length of teacher and student day; calendar)

5. School Goals

- Exit infrastructure (different types of diplomas; different types of programs such as Advanced Scholars, Vocational, Tech Prep, etc.)
- Strategic plan

6. School Budget

- Total staff budget (administrative, certified, non-certified)
- Total school-controlled operating budget
- Total school-controlled instructional budget (separate by source: local district, Title 1, grants, etc.)
- Individual teacher salaries and benefits, including days of employment (w/vacation, etc.)
- Individual staff salaries and benefits, including days of employment (w/vacation, etc.)
- Individual administrator salaries and benefits, including days of employment (w/vacation, etc.)

About the Authors

Marilyn Crawford is an educational consultant working with Education Trust, an international consulting firm called Certain Knowledge, and school leaders and districts across the country. She earned a Ph.D. from Vanderbilt University in Educational Leadership and has extensive public school experience as a teacher, principal, and central office coordinator. Other publications include *The Productive High School* (Corwin Press, with coauthor with Joseph Murphy) and *Learning in Overdrive* (Fulcrum Press, with Ruth Mitchell).

Eleanor Dougherty is senior associate with Education Trust, a nonprofit organization in Washington, D.C. that serves education communities in their efforts to improve student achievement for all students. She has experience as an elementary and secondary teacher, as well as teaching in colleges and universities. For the last several years, she has worked with high-poverty districts around the country in standards-based reforms. She is the author of *Shifting Gears: Standards, Assessments, Curriculum and Instruction* and articles on education.